D0575260

Series Titles

Prehistory	I	XIII	Settling the Americas
Mesopotamia and the Bible Lands	II	XIV	Asian and African Empires
Ancient Egypt and Greece	III	XV	The Industrial Revolution
The Roman World	IV	XVI	Enlightenment and Revolution
Asian Civilizations	V	XVII	Nationalism and the Romantic Movement
Americas and the Pacific	VI	XVIII	The Age of Empire
Early Medieval Times	VII	XIX	North America: Expansion, Civil War, and Emergence
Beyond Europe	VIII	XX	Turn of the Century and the Great War
Late Medieval Europe	IX	XXI	Versailles to World War II
Renaissance Europe	X	XXII	1945 to the Cold War
Voyages of Discovery	XI	XXIII	1991 to the 21st Century
Birth of Modern Nations	XII	XXIV	Issues Today

This Zak Books edition was published 2009.

Zak Books is an imprint of McRae Books.

PREHISTORY

was created and produced by McRae Books Srl

Via del Salviatino, 1 — 50016 — Fiesole (Florence), (Italy)

info@mcraebooks.com

www.mcraebooks.com

Publishers: Anne McRae, Marco Nardi

Series Editor: Anne McRae

Author: Neil Morris

Main Illustrations: Valeria Ferretti pp. 16–17, 24–25, 38–39; MM comunicazione (Manuela Cappon, Monica Favilli) pp. 40–41; Francesca D'Ottavi pp. 42–43, 44; Antonella Pastorelli p. 19; Paola Ravaglia pp. 36–37; Sergio pp. 20–21, 22–23, 28–29, 32–33; Studio Stalio (Ivan Stalio, Alessandro Cantucci, Fabiano Fabbrucci, Margherita Salvadori) pp. 7, 8–9, 10–11, 12–13, 14–15

Smaller Illustrations: Studio Stalio (Alessandro Cantucci, Fabiano Fabbrucci, Margherita Salvadori)

Maps: Paola Baldanzi

Photos: Bridgeman Art Library, London/Farabola Foto, Milan p.30t; Corbis/Contrasto, Milan pp. 26b, 34–35

Art Director: Marco Nardi

Layouts: Rebecca Milner

Project Editor: Loredana Agosta

Research: Valerie Meek, Claire Moore, Loredana Agosta

Repro: Litocolor, Florence

Consultants: Dr. Ken Mowbray and Dr. Ian Tattersall

Dr. Tattersall is Curator of the Department of Anthropology at the American Museum of Natural History and adjunct professor of anthropology at Columbia University. Trained in archaeology, anthropology, geology and paleontology, he has carried out fieldwork in many countries and is the author of numerous publications.

Dr. Mowbray is Curatorial Associate of the Department Anthropology at the American Museum of Natural History. A widely travelled paleoanthropologist, Dr. Mowbray has examined some of the world's greatest fossil finds and has written and/or collaborated on numerous publications in scientific journals.

Library of Congress Cataloging-in-Publication Data

Morris, Neil, 1946-

Prehistory / Neil Morris.

p. cm. -- (History of the world)

Summary: "A detailed overview of history from the beginning of the world to when humans began to record their history, including archaeological evidence for what we know about prehistory"--Provided by publisher.

Includes index.

ISBN 978-8860981561

1. Prehistoric peoples--Juvenile literature. 2. Earth--History--Juvenile literature. I. Title.

GN744.M67 2009

930--dc22

2008008399

Printed and bound in Malaysia.

Prehistory

Neil Morris

Consultants: Dr. Ian Tattersall, Curator of the Department of Anthropology at the American Museum of Natural History
Dr. Ken Mowbray, Curatorial Associate of the Department of Anthropology at the American Museum of Natural History

Zak BOOKS

Contents

Note—This book shows dates as related to the conventional beginning of our era, or the year 1, understood as the year of the birth of Jesus Christ. All events dating before this year are listed as BCE (Before Current Era). Events dating after the year 1 are defined as CE (Current Era).

TIMELINES

EARTH'S HISTORY

Precambrian			Palaeozoic					
Hadean 4.6–3.8 billion years ago	Archean 3.8–2.6 billion years ago	Proterozoic 2.6 billion–590 million years ago	Cambrian 590–505 million years ago	Ordovician 505–434 million years ago	Silurian 434–408 million years ago	Devonian 408–354 million years ago	Carboniferous 354–286 million years ago	Perm 248 r years
The Earth forms as a molten mass.	The Earth cools and the first forms of life appear.	Multi-celled animals appear, including trilobites.	Jellyfish, sponges and shelled animals live in shallow seas.	The Earth's land mass is made up of one supercontinent, Pangaea. Mollusks, starfish, and corals are abundant in the sea.	The Earth's temperature stabilizes and plants appear on land. Fish develop jaws.	Fish dominate sea life; amphibians and insects appear on land.	Reptiles appear; large swampy forests cover the land; there are giant flying insects.	Mammal-like reptiles and seed plants appear, with conifers dominant. Mass extinction at the end of Permian.

HUMAN HISTORY

	7 million years ago		5 million years ago		3 million years ago	
EARLY HOMINIDS	*Sahelanthropus tchadensis*	*Orrorin tugenensis*	*Australopithecus anamensis*	*Australopithecus afarensis*	*Australopithecus africanus*; *Paranthropus aethiopicus*; *Homo rudolfensis*; *Paranthropus boisei*	*Homo erectus*; *Homo habilis*; *Homo ergaster*
MODERN HUMANS						

Introduction

The earliest metal objects, dating from around 5000 BCE, were produced by hammering. These golden bull ornaments were found at a grave site in Bulgaria.

The term "prehistory" refers to the history of the world from its very beginnings to the time when our ancestors first started keeping written records. Life began in the warm waters of the Earth and followed a succession of different forms, from single-celled animals through dinosaurs to the first mammals. They were followed by the first human-like creatures, called hominids, who learned to use tools and control the use of fire. After modern humans first appeared more than 130,000 years ago, they gradually colonized the planet and dominated its resources. Some hunter-gatherer groups eventually took up farming and began to settle in one place. As their numbers grew, these prehistoric people were able to devote some of their time to art, religion and trade. Simple settlements grew into impressive cities, leading to the beginning of modern civilization. More than 5,000 years ago, people invented writing systems and started keeping records, marking the end of the prehistoric period.

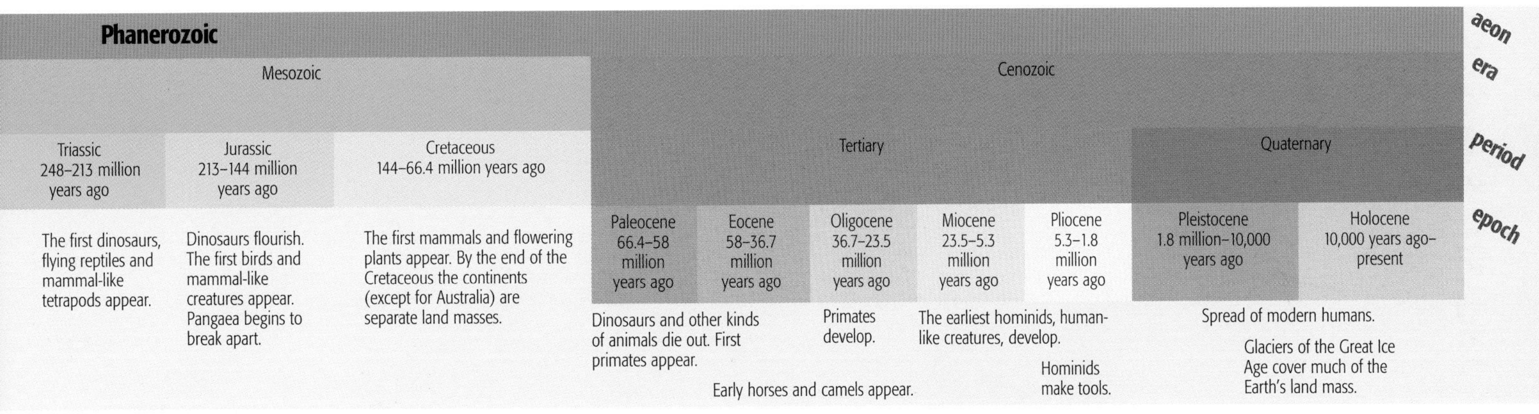

1 million years ago

Homo neanderthalensis

Homo sapiens

8000 BCE

Farming begins in Mesopotamia.

Foundation of Çatal Hüyük.

6000 BCE

Farming begins in southern Europe and in the Indus Valley.

Megalithic monuments are built in Europe.

4000 BCE

Farming begins in Central America.

Egyptians use hieroglyphics.

Villages appear in South America.

2000 BCE

Minoans begin to write.

Chinese use pictographs.

As the fireball went on expanding but started to cool, hydrogen and helium came together. The force of gravity compressed the gases into galaxies, each of which was made up of billions of stars.

The Big Bang

According to the most widely held theory, all matter existed in a microscopic particle at the beginning of time. The Big Bang then caused this dense particle to expand with incredible energy and speed. The explosion was so enormous that less than a minute later the resulting Universe was many millions of miles across. It also produced an incredibly hot fireball that started nuclear reactions and created elements such as hydrogen and helium.

One of the chemical substances that formed was deoxyribonucleic acid, or DNA. Made up of two strands like a spiral ladder, DNA has the ability to make copies of itself. These copies generate proteins which aid in making up every living thing on the planet.

In the Beginning

Most scientists believe that the Universe began with a Big Bang, around 15 billion years ago. Millions of years later, as the Universe continued to expand, clouds of gas and dust clumped together to form galaxies full of stars. Rocky planets arose around one such star, in a spiral galaxy that we call the Milky Way, and it was on one of these planets that life would eventually form. The star was our Sun and the planet was Earth. As the red-hot planet cooled, oceans formed around its land masses. Many millions of years were to pass before the most primitive forms of life developed.

HEAVENLY BODIES

c. 15 billion years ago
Origin of the Universe with the Big Bang – a term coined by British cosmologist Sir Fred Hoyle (1915–2001) in 1950.

c. 4.6 billion years ago
The Sun forms in a spiral galaxy that we call the Milky Way (which contains at least 100 billion stars). It is made up mainly of hydrogen, with smaller amounts of other gases and traces of metals.

c. 4.6 billion years ago
Formation of planet Earth within the Solar System. It is about 92,960,000 miles (150 million km) away from the Sun. It travels around the Sun once every 365.25 days.

c. 4.4 billion years ago
Formation of the Moon (a satellite of Earth), probably from bits of material after another planetary body crashed into the Earth. It is 239,900 miles (384,400 km) away from the Earth. It travels around the Earth once every 27.32 days.

The Solar System

As galaxies formed, great whirls of gas and dust came together to make stars. This was how our Sun came into being, about 4.6 billion years ago. At the same time, bits of dust that were circling around the new star collided and slowed down. They came together to make lumps that grew into rocky spheres–the inner planets of our Solar System. Further away from the Sun, gas came together to form four large planets. Pluto, previously known as the ninth planet, is now considered to be a dwarf planet, along with several other small, distant objects made of rock and ice.

Along with seven other major planets, the Earth orbits around the Sun.

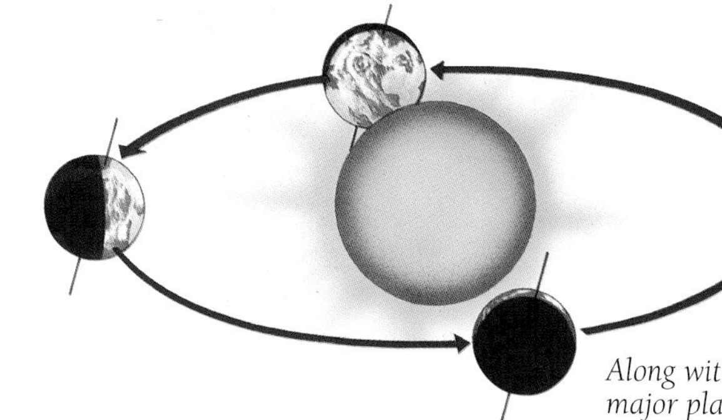

The bits of dust and rocky particles in the early Solar System were of different sizes. They went on crashing into each other and being pulled together by gravity until they formed planets, such as the Earth and the Moon.

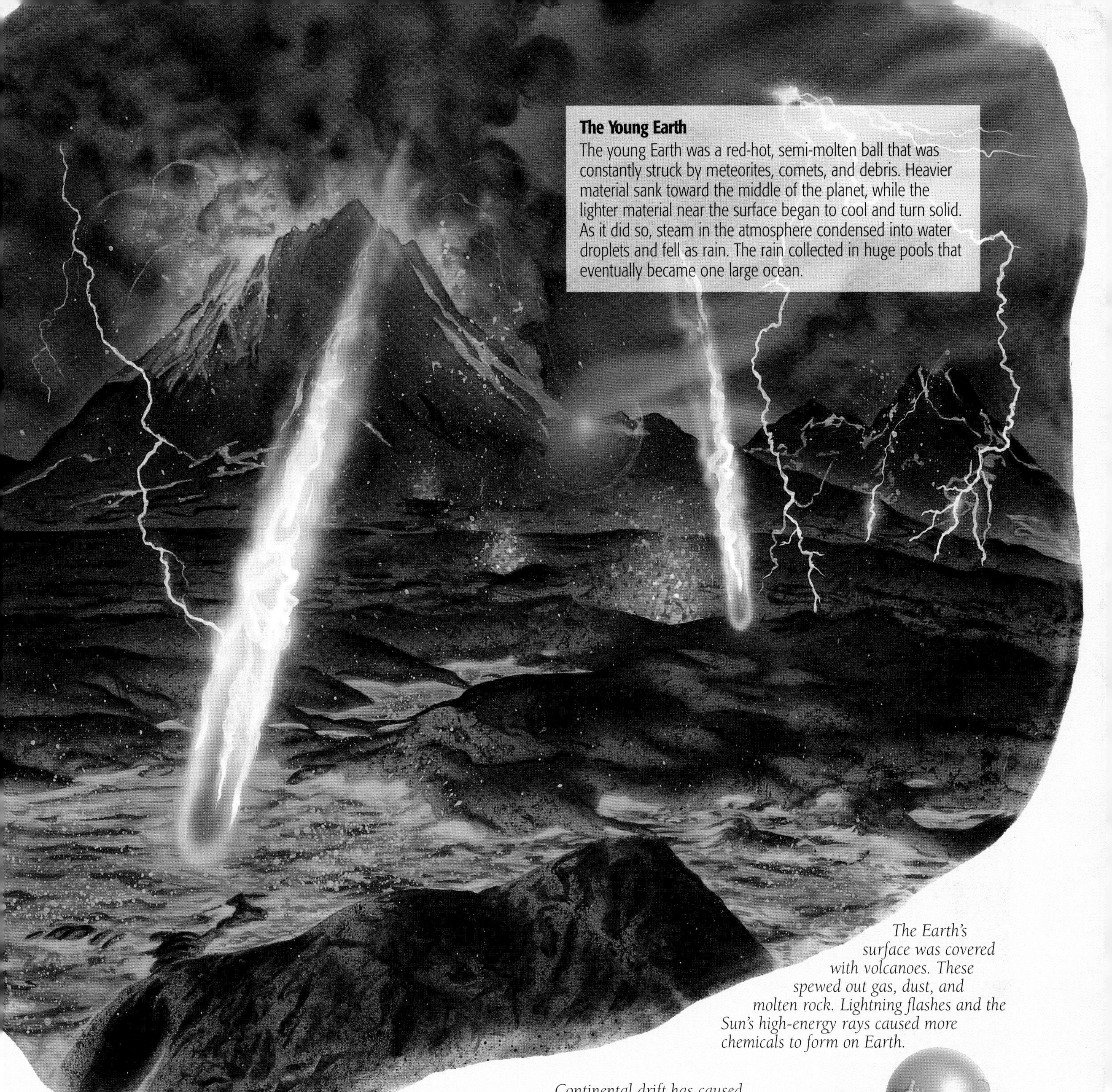

The Young Earth

The young Earth was a red-hot, semi-molten ball that was constantly struck by meteorites, comets, and debris. Heavier material sank toward the middle of the planet, while the lighter material near the surface began to cool and turn solid. As it did so, steam in the atmosphere condensed into water droplets and fell as rain. The rain collected in huge pools that eventually became one large ocean.

The Earth's surface was covered with volcanoes. These spewed out gas, dust, and molten rock. Lightning flashes and the Sun's high-energy rays caused more chemicals to form on Earth.

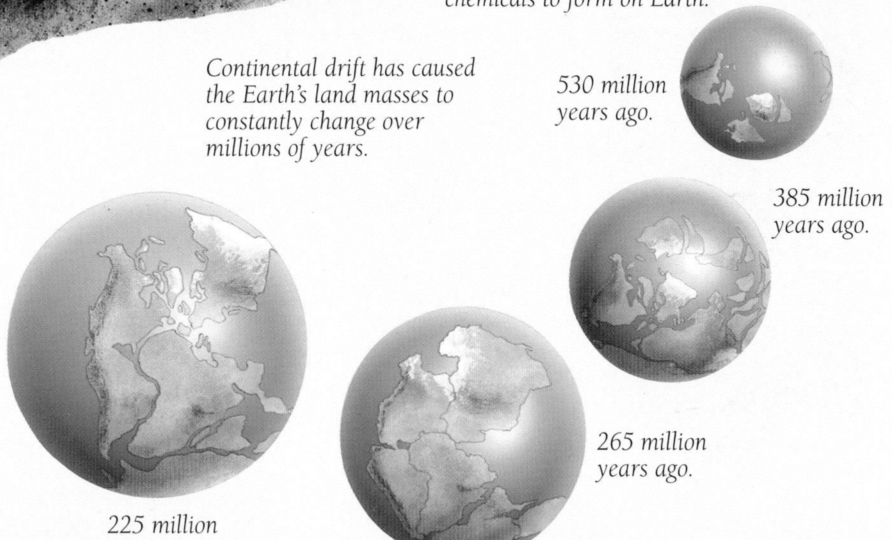

Continental drift has caused the Earth's land masses to constantly change over millions of years.

530 million years ago.

Continental Drift

The Earth's crust, or solid outer layer, is cracked into huge pieces, called plates. Hundreds of millions of years ago, the continental plates that made up the Earth's land began drifting together. By about 265 million years ago they joined up to form a single supercontinent called Pangaea. Then, around 200–225 million years ago, the supercontinent began to break up and land masses slowly started moving apart. This slow movement, called continental drift, still continues today.

385 million years ago.

265 million years ago.

225 million years ago.

Early Forms of Life

The first long span of geological time, which we call the Precambrian eon, covers more than 4 billion years, or nearly nine-tenths of the whole history of the Earth. The planet's oceans, continents, and atmosphere changed considerably during that enormous time span. Simple, single-celled forms of life developed in the warm water and soft mud that were found at the edge of shallow seas. Later, more complex animals developed—also in the sea—until there was an explosion of life during the Cambrian period. By the end of this period, about 500 million years ago, the shallow seas were teeming with jellyfish, sponges, and the first shelled animals.

Precambrian Beginnings
Earth changed continually during the long Precambrian eon. The solid surface had cooled enough for ice to form, and there were at least three Precambrian ice ages. Nevertheless, a "soup" of chemicals continued to grow in warm shallow seas, leading eventually to the development of the first living cells. These were simple, single-celled organisms similar to the microscopic bacteria that are still alive today. Some forms, known as blue-green algae, gathered together to form mounds called stromatolites.

Stromatolites are created when the sticky mucus produced by blue-green algae traps sand, dust and chemicals in seawater, forming rings of limestone in the shallow sea. Stromatolites continue to form today off the coast of Australia.

Early Life Forms
During the Precambrian eon, simple organisms such as blue-green algae started using the hydrogen in water and giving off oxygen. This enormous development was the beginning of photosynthesis, the process by which plants produce their own food today. During the last era of the Precambrian eon, the amount of oxygen in the atmosphere started to increase and a large number of different multi-celled, soft-bodied life forms developed.

Fossil of the Spriggina, a Precambrian worm-like animal, named after the finder of its fossil, the geologist Sir Reginald Sprigg (1919–1994).

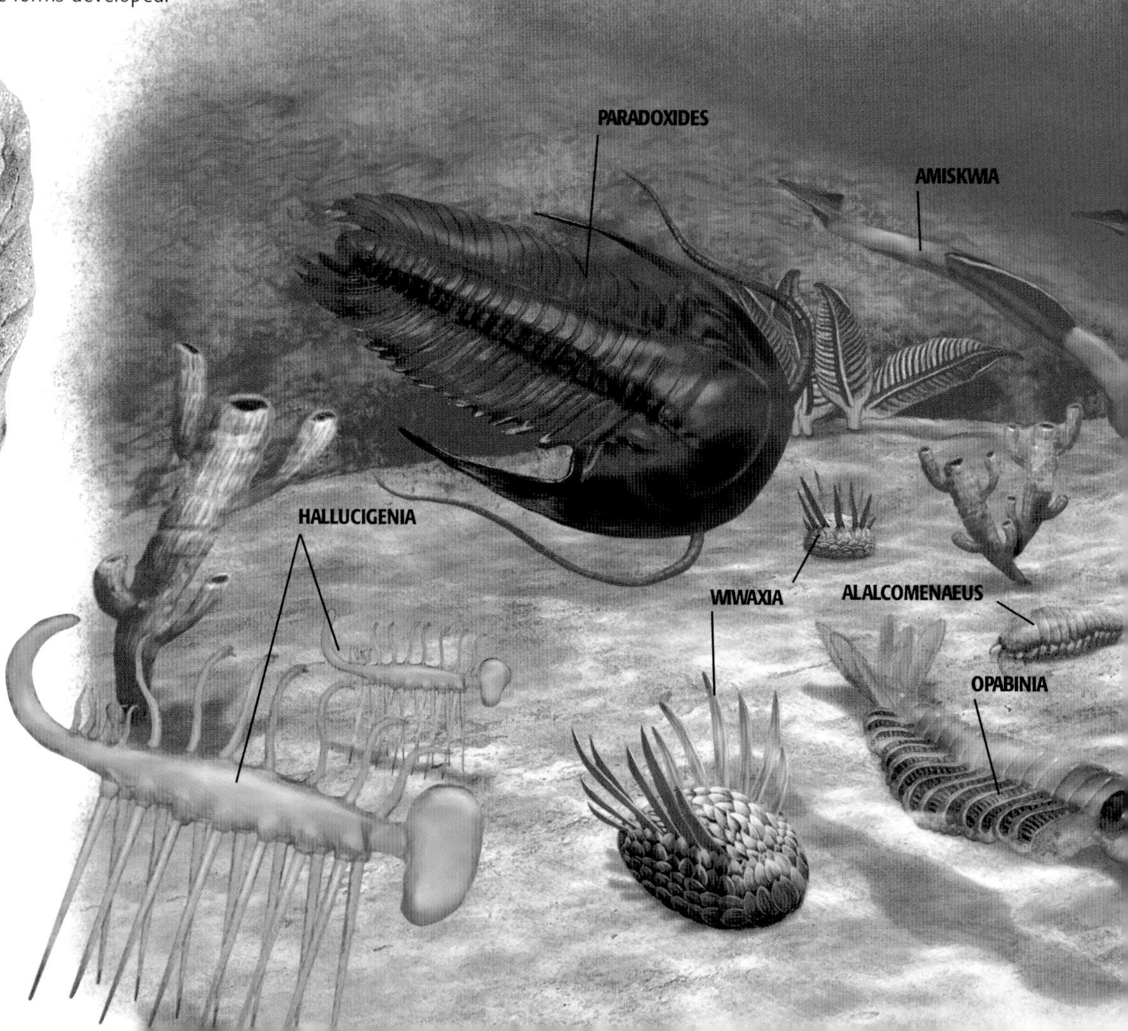

PARADOXIDES
AMISKWIA
HALLUCIGENIA
WIWAXIA
ALALCOMENAEUS
OPABINIA

The Cambrian Explosion

There was an explosion of new life forms early in the Cambrian period. Many of the major groups of animals that we know today appeared at that time. Some of the new life forms developed exoskeletons (shells) to protect their soft bodies. One of the most famous groups was made up of trilobites, which had a flat oval body divided into three sections and large curved eyes. Trilobites lived on the seabed, and some also swam in the waters above. They died out about 245 million years ago.

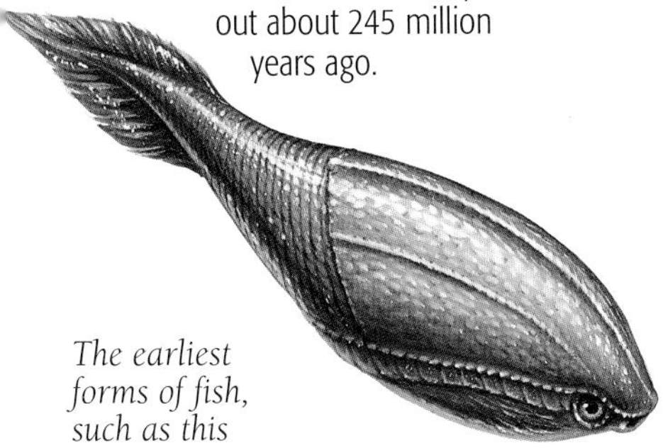

The earliest forms of fish, such as this Arandapis, *were covered in bony plates. They had no jaws, no body fins, and no internal bones.*

Different kinds of jellyfish developed in the late Precambrian.

Fossil of a trilobite, showing clearly the three segments of its shell.

An Extraordinary Discovery

In 1909, fossils of Cambrian life forms were found in a bed of shale (soft rock made of hardened mud) in the Rocky Mountains, in Canada. The fossils in this shale, known as the Burgess shale, revealed the forms of a large number of soft-bodied animals that lived in the warm, shallow, early Cambrian waters of what is now North America. The animals seem to have been buried by a mudslide. Then, over the course of many millions of years, their remains turned into fossils.

GEOLOGICAL TIME

Geological time, or Earth's history, is divided into two eons, the Precambrian and the Phanerozoic (see timeline on pages 4–5). The Phanerozoic eon is divided into three eras–Paleozoic, Mesozoic and Cenozoic–which are further divided into periods. The first period of the Paleozoic era is the Cambrian period. It was named in 1835 by Adam Sedgwick (1785–1873), a Cambridge professor of geology who studied a Welsh layer of shale and sandstone rocks. He referred to them by the Latin name for Wales, Cambria. Everything before that time was then called Precambrian. The Ordovician and Silurian periods were named after ancient Celtic tribes in Wales, because fossils from those times were found there. The Devonian refers to the English county of Devon. The name Carboniferous, given by two British scientists in 1822, refers to the carbon present in rocks of that period. Permian was named after the Perm region of the Ural Mountains in Russia.

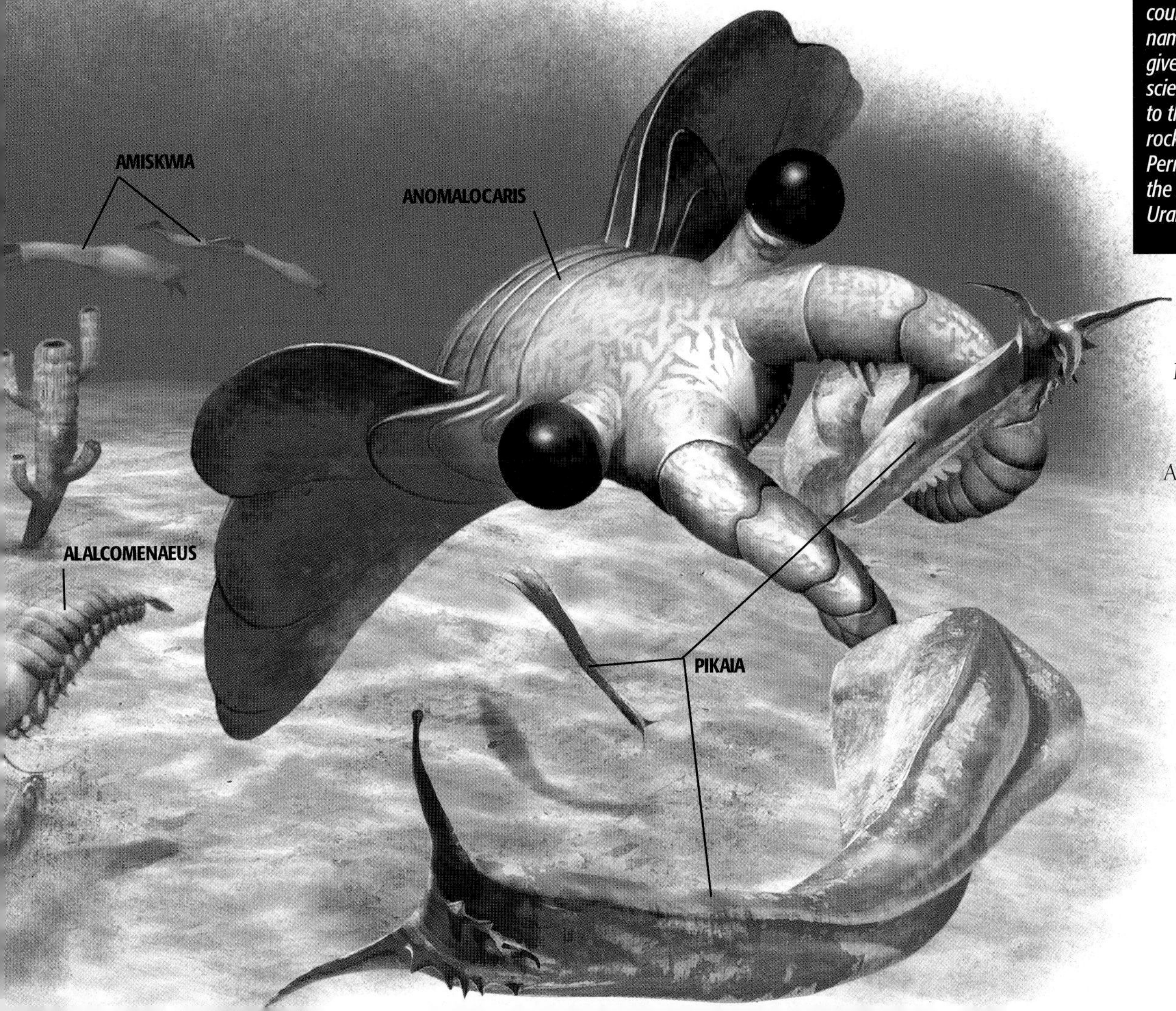

AMISKWIA

ANOMALOCARIS

ALALCOMENAEUS

PIKAIA

The animals of the Burgess shale included trilobites such as the Paradoxides, *a large predator called* Anomalocaris, *and the* Wiwaxia, *which were worm-like creatures covered with spines.*

Evolution of Species

Life on Earth went though tremendous change during the 250 million years following the Cambrian period. Fish and other marine creatures continued to develop, but the greatest change involved life moving on to land. The first amphibians appeared, to be followed by land-based reptiles, some of which developed features that were similar to the mammals that would follow later. Plants grew on land, and insects spread rapidly as large swampy forests appeared. But just as the number and variety of species increased, there were also great setbacks. These included three periods of mass extinction, the greatest of which occurred at the very end of the era.

Devonian fossil of a small fish with muscular paired fins.

The Age of Fish

Fish developed jaws and became abundant in freshwater rivers and lakes. They dominated the oceans during the Devonian (408–354 million years ago), a period within the Paleozoic era which is often called the "age of fish." Some early bony fish had fleshy lobed fins, which they used to crawl along the seabed. Other species had rayed fins and were fast swimmers, and these included the first sharks.

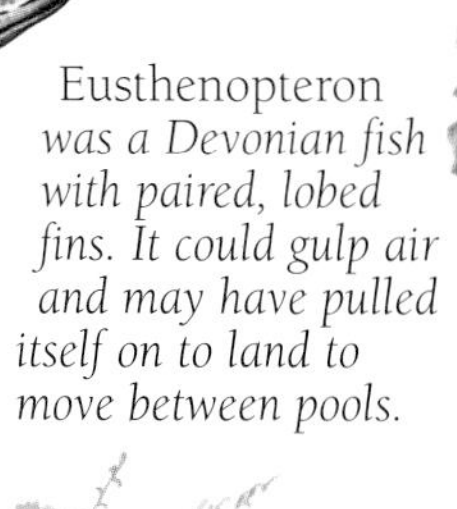

Eusthenopteron *was a Devonian fish with paired, lobed fins. It could gulp air and may have pulled itself on to land to move between pools.*

Tree ferns became common during the Carboniferous period.

Early Reptiles

During the late Devonian period, some sea creatures crawled out on to land. These amphibians, like frogs and toads today, were able to lead a "double life" —on land and in water. They were followed by the first reptiles. These were small, lizard-like animals that laid their leathery-shelled eggs on land, whereas amphibians laid their soft eggs in water. The reptiles could spend all their time on land, where spreading forests were helping to increase the amount of oxygen in the atmosphere.

The Permian landscape was dominated by amphibians, reptiles and mammal-like reptiles. Some were plant-eaters, and the earliest flying reptiles took to the air. Other reptiles, called mesosaurs, went back to the water.

LYCAENOPS

CEOLUROSAURAVUS

PELTOBATRACHUS

Leading to Mammals

During the Permian period, amphibians and reptiles were joined on land by a group of animals that we call mammal-like reptiles. Some were quite small, but others grew as large as a modern rhinoceros. One group, the cynodonts, developed different kinds of teeth and a bony shelf in the roof of the mouth that allowed them to eat and breathe at the same time. Their limbs were more like later mammals, and they may even have had fur to keep them warm.

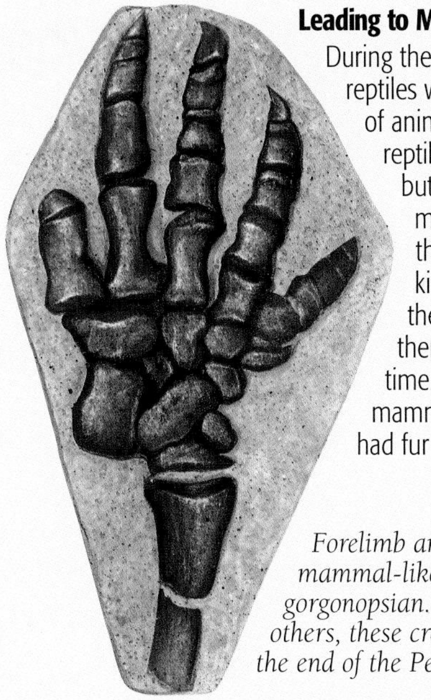

Forelimb and foot of a mammal-like reptile called a gorgonopsian. Along with many others, these creatures died out at the end of the Permian period.

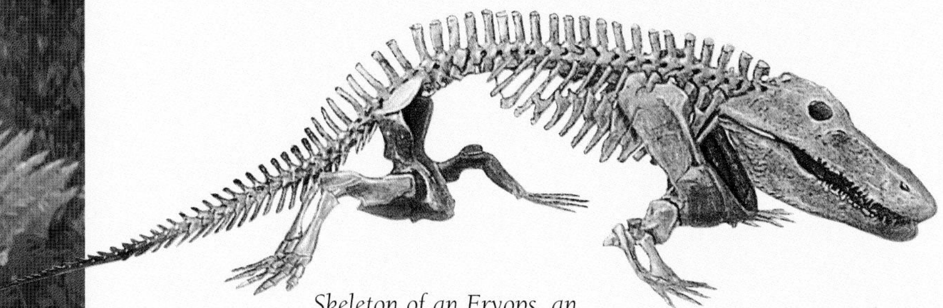

Skeleton of an Eryops, an amphibian of the Permian period, measuring 6.5 feet (2 m) long. It probably fed mainly in the water, catching fish and smaller amphibians.

Mass Extinction

At the end of the Permian period an enormous number of animals died out –up to 95 percent of those that we know from the fossil record. There had been two earlier mass extinctions, but the Permian was the biggest the Earth has ever known. It almost wiped out the mammal-like reptiles, and more than three-quarters of land-based vertebrates were lost, along with half of all plant species. Even more species became extinct in the sea. Scientists believe a dramatic event caused the mass extinction. There are several possible causes: a gigantic asteroid or comet may have struck the Earth; or perhaps there were vast volcanic eruptions; and there might have been great changes in global climate and sea levels.

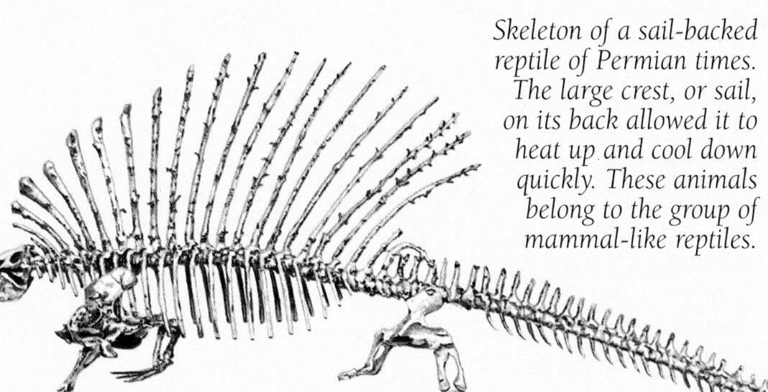

Skeleton of a sail-backed reptile of Permian times. The large crest, or sail, on its back allowed it to heat up and cool down quickly. These animals belong to the group of mammal-like reptiles.

The Age of Dinosaurs

Scientists divide the Mesozoic era, which began about 248 million years ago, into three periods—the Triassic, the Jurassic, and the Cretaceous. Reptiles known as dinosaurs emerged during the first of these periods and dominated life on land for roughly 165 million years, before dying out completely at the end of the era. The dinosaurs were a wide-ranging group of animals. Some were gigantic, others quite small. Some plant-eaters moved around in herds, while most meat-eaters probably hunted alone. At the same time there were many other animals in the air and in the sea.

DINOSAURS IN THE MESOZOIC

Key: dinosaur name, time span, body length, diet, fossil location.

TRIASSIC AGE:
Eoraptor
228 million years ago, 3.3 feet (1 m), meat, Argentina.

Herrerasaurus
228 million years ago, 10 feet (3 m), meat, Argentina.

Coelophysis
225–220 million years ago, 10 feet (3 m), meat, USA.

Plateosaurus
210 million years ago, 23 feet (7 m), plants, Europe.

JURASSIC AGE:
Anchisaurus
190 million years ago, 6.5 feet (2 m), plants, USA.

Megalosaurus
170–155 million years ago, 30 feet (9 m), meat, England.

Apatosaurus
154–145 million years ago, 69 feet (21 m), plants, USA.

Archaeopteryx
147 million years ago, 1.5 feet (50 cm), meat, Germany.

CRETACEOUS AGE:
Iguanodon
140–110 million years ago, 33 feet (10 m), plants, Europe.

Oviraptor
85–75 million years ago, 6 feet (1.8 m), meat and plants, Mongolia.

Hadrosaurus
78–74 million years ago, 30 feet (9 m), plants, USA.

Triceratops
67–65 million years ago, 30 feet (9 m), plants, USA.

Fossilized dinosaur eggs. Female dinosaurs laid leathery, hard-shelled eggs, probably in mud nests or hollows.

What is a Dinosaur?

Though their name means "terrible lizard," dinosaurs were only distantly related to lizards (and many were not very terrible!). Scientists divide them into two groups, according to the structure of their hips. Saurischians, which had hips shaped like those of modern lizards, included herbivores and carnivores. The second and later group, called ornithischians, had hips like a bird's, and were all herbivores. Some dinosaurs walked on four legs, others on two.

Some reptiles took to the air during the late Triassic. The Eudimorphodon *(shown here), had a long tail and a short neck.*

Early Species

The first saurischian dinosaurs emerged during the Triassic period. The earliest were probably all carnivores, such as the bipedal *Coelophysis*. By the end of the period, there were also much larger herbivores, such as the *Riojasaurus*, and dinosaurs were spreading out as the Earth's land masses began drifting apart.

Supremacy on Land

During the Jurassic period dinosaurs flourished and took over the Earth's spreading continents. Ferns, mosses, cycads, and conifers thrived, providing food for the growing number of herbivores. Many herbivores, such as *Diplodocus*, grew very large, providing them with some protection against meat-eating species. Others developed bony plates and other armor. *Stegosaurus* and its cousins had pointed tail spikes, which could inflict damage on any attacking carnivore.

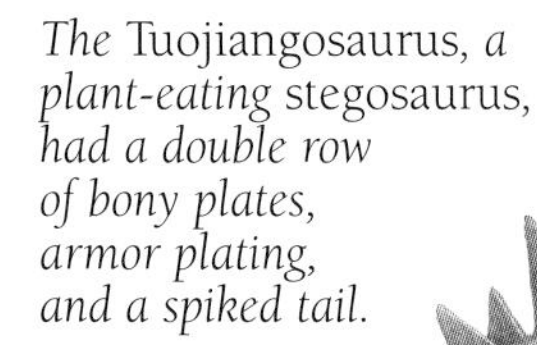

The Tuojiangosaurus*, a plant-eating* stegosaurus*, had a double row of bony plates, armor plating, and a spiked tail.*

The Cretaceous World

The range of dinosaurs continued to grow throughout the Cretaceous period, as the continents continued to split apart. Great layers of chalk were laid down as the oceans advanced over shallow continental shelves. Marine reptiles, such as *Plesiosaurs*, thrived, and there were flowering plants on land. Some of the most famous dinosaurs came to prominence, such as the fierce carnivorous *Tyrannosaurs* and the duck-billed herbivorous *Hadrosaurs*.

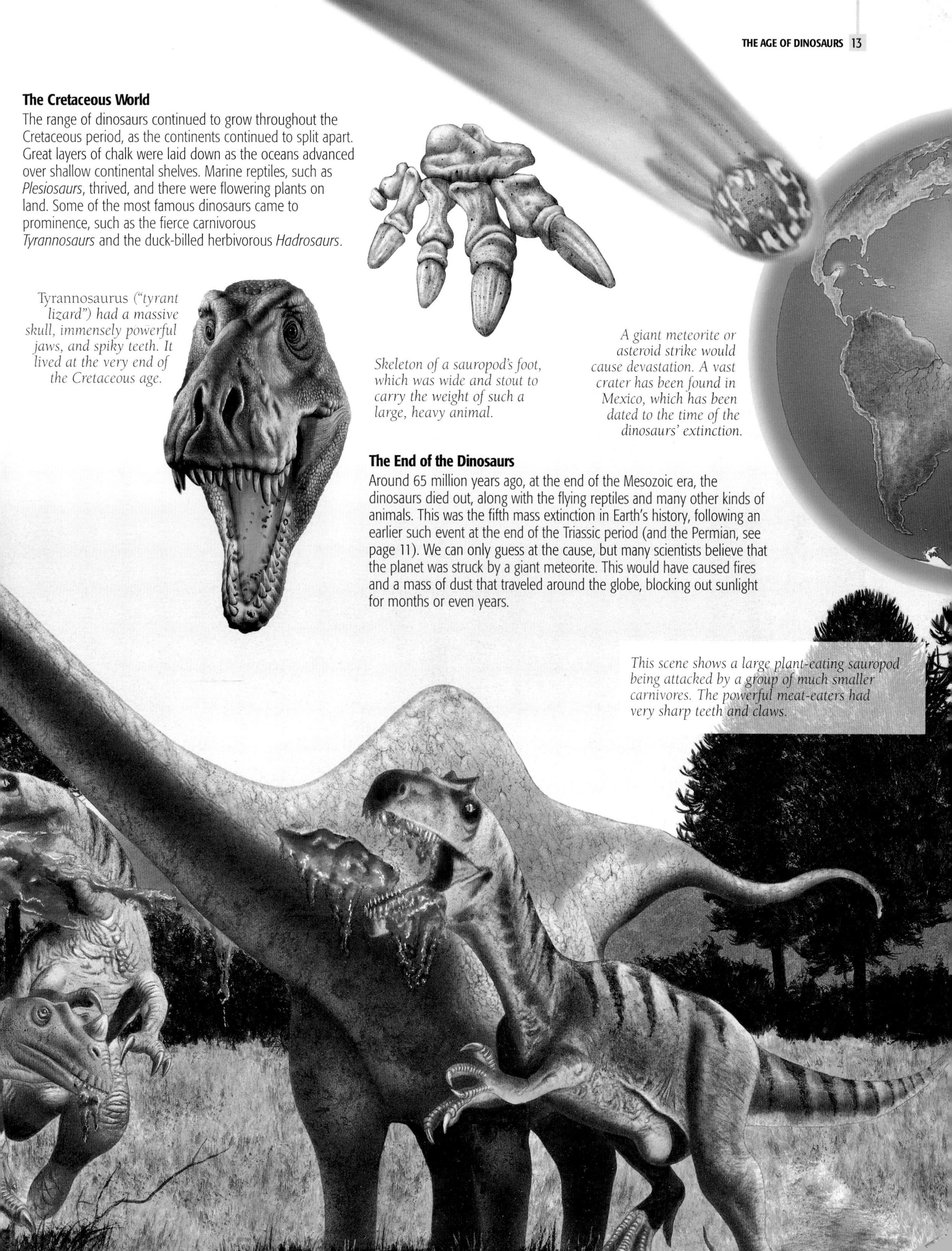

Tyrannosaurus *("tyrant lizard") had a massive skull, immensely powerful jaws, and spiky teeth. It lived at the very end of the Cretaceous age.*

Skeleton of a sauropod's foot, which was wide and stout to carry the weight of such a large, heavy animal.

A giant meteorite or asteroid strike would cause devastation. A vast crater has been found in Mexico, which has been dated to the time of the dinosaurs' extinction.

The End of the Dinosaurs

Around 65 million years ago, at the end of the Mesozoic era, the dinosaurs died out, along with the flying reptiles and many other kinds of animals. This was the fifth mass extinction in Earth's history, following an earlier such event at the end of the Triassic period (and the Permian, see page 11). We can only guess at the cause, but many scientists believe that the planet was struck by a giant meteorite. This would have caused fires and a mass of dust that traveled around the globe, blocking out sunlight for months or even years.

This scene shows a large plant-eating sauropod being attacked by a group of much smaller carnivores. The powerful meat-eaters had very sharp teeth and claws.

MAMMAL FACTS

Mammal Birth
Three different kinds of mammals evolved: monotremes, which lay eggs (e.g. modern platypus); marsupials, which give birth to undeveloped young (e.g. koala); placentals, which give birth to more advanced young (and include most modern mammals).

Mammalian Characteristics
All mammals have a backbone and body hair or fur to keep warm; they are warm-blooded, so keep a constant body temperature; the lower jaw is a single bone, and there are three small bones in the middle ear; females feed young on their own milk; different teeth are shaped for different jobs.

A small Saltopus *dinosaur of the late Triassic has caught a* Morganucodon, *a tiny insect-eater that was one of the first true mammals.*

Skeleton of Mesohippus, *an early three-toed horse that lived during the Oligocene epoch.*

The Age of Mammals

Mammals first appeared during the Mesozoic era, having evolved from the so-called mammal-like reptiles. Their small size and burrowing habits may have helped them survive the events that caused the extinction of the dinosaurs. The mammals went on to thrive during the Tertiary period, which is often called the Age of Mammals. Carnivores, rodents, hoofed animals, elephants, and primates all emerged, adapting well to changing conditions on different continents. As in earlier periods, there was not a straight line of evolution that led from one species to another. Many of the early kinds of mammal died out, and we know of them only from fossil finds.

Early Species

The first, small mammal-like creatures of the late Triassic period (around 213 million years ago) probably lived in dense foliage or burrows and were active only at night. These tiny, shrew-like animals remained small during the rest of the Mesozoic era and fell prey to meat-eating dinosaurs. Nevertheless, more groups of mammals had developed by the time the dinosaurs died out. After their extinction, there was more food available and mammals started coming out in the day. Many groups were egg-laying monotremes, which are represented today by the spiny anteater and platypus of Australia.

This imaginary scene shows a timeline of mammal evolution.

PALEOCENE **EOCENE**

Marsupials

The group of mammals called marsupials give birth to less developed young, which spend their early life in a pouch of skin on their mother's abdomen. The early marsupials spread to most continents during the Eocene epoch, but today almost all of them live in Australia and South America.

A female kangaroo, one of the marsupial mammals, with a young joey in her pouch.

Wide-Ranging Evolution

Soon after the start of the Tertiary period, mammals started evolving into different shapes and sizes. By the time of the Eocene epoch, the continents were moving to the positions they occupy today. At that time large herbivores emerged, including the ancestors of the camel, horse, and rhinoceros. Among smaller mammals, the first rodents appeared. Mammals even took to the water and the air, in the form of the first whales and bats.

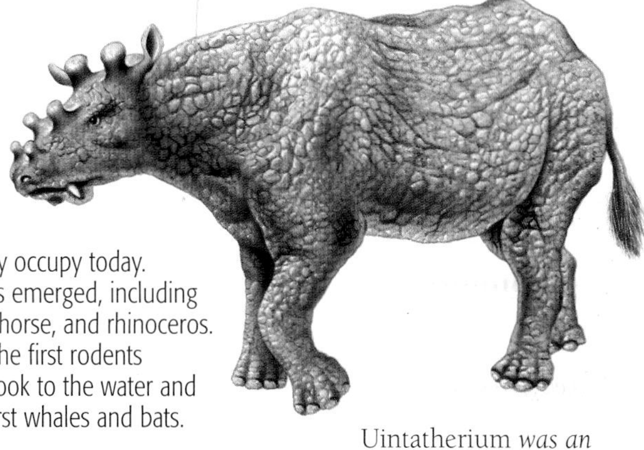

Uintatherium *was an early large herbivore of the Eocene epoch. About the size of a modern rhinoceros, it ate leaves.*

Skeleton of Smilodectes, *a tree-climbing primate that lived about 50 million years ago.*

Placentals

Placental mammals are much more developed when they are born than marsupials. They are nourished in their mother's uterus by an organ called the placenta. They evolved into the largest and most successful group of mammals, spreading to all parts of the world and adapting well to different climates and habitats. There are about 4,000 species alive today.

Fossil of a mouse-like creature, dated to 125 million years ago, which scientists think may have been the first placental mammal.

Primates

The primates (a word meaning "of the first rank") are considered to be the highest order of mammals. Today the group includes prosimians, monkeys, apes, and humans. The earliest primates appeared during the Paleocene epoch, and by about 50 million years ago they had the characteristic features of grasping hands, short snout, eyes at the front of the head, and an enlarged brain area.

PLATYBELODON

INDRICOTHERIUM

NIMRAVUS

CLADOSICTIS

PACHYRUKHOS

OLIGOCENE **MIOCENE**

HOMINID FAMILY TREE

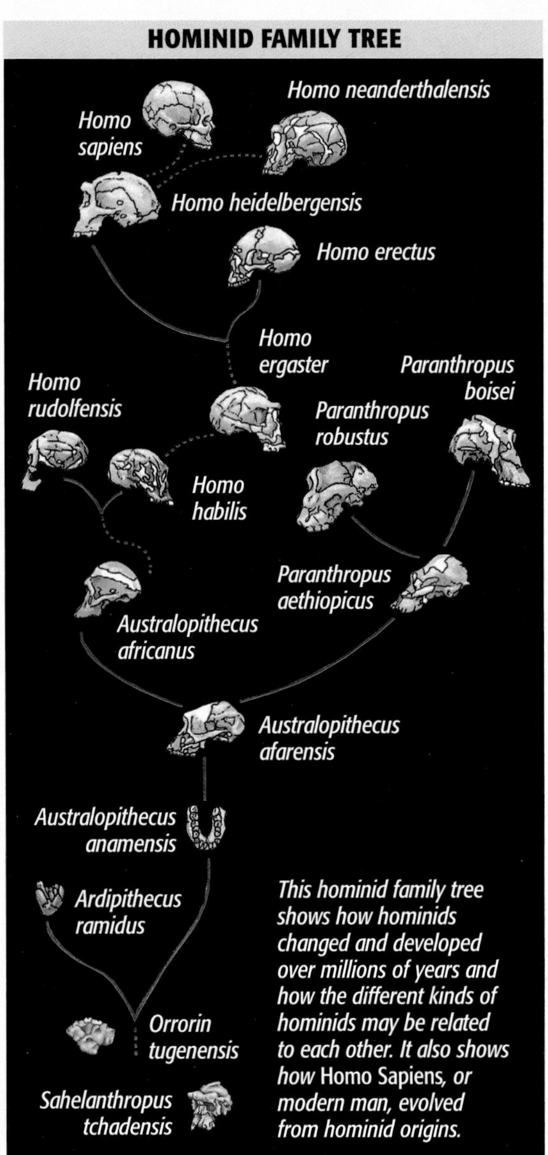

This hominid family tree shows how hominids changed and developed over millions of years and how the different kinds of hominids may be related to each other. It also shows how Homo Sapiens*, or modern man, evolved from hominid origins.*

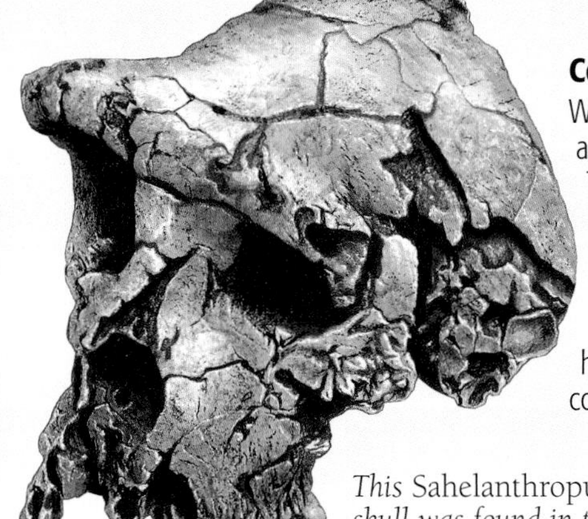

This Sahelanthropus tchadensis *skull was found in the African country of Chad and nicknamed Toumaï, meaning "hope of life."*

Common Ancestors

Within the order of primates, the first apes appeared about 25 million years ago. Today the family of so-called "great apes" (officially called *Pongidae*) includes chimpanzees, gorillas, and orangutans. At some distant point in the past, the great apes and the earliest human-like creatures, hominids, shared a common ancestor.

The First Hominids

In 2000, fossilized bone fragments of an early hominid were found in Kenya. It was given the species name *Orrorin tugenensis* and dated to 6 million years ago. Two years later, a French scientist announced the discovery of an even older hominid skull. It was given the species name *Sahelanthropus tchadensis* and found to be nearly 7 million years old. Its discoverer thinks that this hominid individual was about the size of a modern chimpanzee.

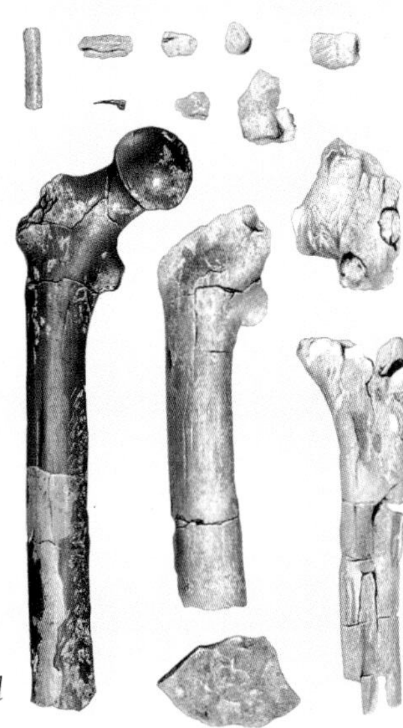

Bone fragments of Orrorin tugenensis*—the hominid also called "Millennium Man"—which were found in Kenya in 2000.*

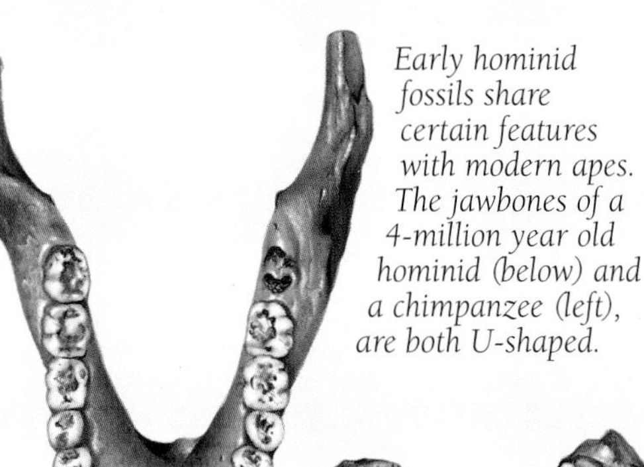

Early hominid fossils share certain features with modern apes. The jawbones of a 4-million year old hominid (below) and a chimpanzee (left), are both U-shaped.

Early Hominids

The first hominids, or human-like creatures, emerged some time between 10 and 5 million years ago. They shared a common ancestor with apes, but had different characteristics. Hominids developed a more upright posture, walked on two legs, and had more rounded skulls and eventually larger brains. Standing upright left their hands free to grasp food, carry it, and defend themselves, as well as allowing them to see further over tall grass and bushes. A group of hominids that we call *Australopithecus* (meaning "southern apes") appeared in Africa about 4 million years ago.

Scientists believe that Australopithecus afarensis *lived in social groups led by the strongest male.*

Australopithecus anamensis lived about 4 million years ago. The fossils below show bone fragments of jaws (top), an arm (center), and a lower leg (bottom).

Many Species

Scientists have found several different *Australopithecus* species. Their craniums were small, about a third of the size of modern humans. The *Homo* group, to which modern humans belong, is believed to have evolved from an *Australopithecus* species (see hominid family tree on page 16).

Living Together

Before the discovery of fossil evidence, scientists thought that only one species of hominid lived at a time. Today we believe that different hominid species, such as *Paranthropus boisei*, *Homo rudolfensis*, *Homo habilis,* and *Homo ergaster* co-existed in what is now northern Kenya about 1.8 million years ago (see timeline on page 4). *Homo habilis* and *Homo rudolfensis* were probably scavengers who may have competed for food.

A female Australopithecus afarensis nursing her young. A partial skeleton of this species, nicknamed "Lucy," was announced in 1974. She lived about 3.2 million years ago in what is now Ethiopia.

Out of Africa

Almost 2 million years ago the first hominids left Africa and migrated to other continents. The migration across the world was not achieved by individuals traveling great distances, but by groups gradually expanding and moving on in search of food. The initial migration, a journey of at least 6,200 miles (10,000 km), may have taken up to 100,000 years. Which of the hominid species was the first to migrate remains a question for modern research to answer.

This is how Homo erectus *("upright man") may have looked. Many "upright" fossils, similar to the African "workmen" have been found in Asia.*

GREAT MIGRATION

Possible migration routes

EUROPE

ASIA

AFRICA

OLDUVAI GORGE

AUSTRALIA

Migrating Species

Some experts believe that the first hominids to migrate were probably Homo ergaster *(or "workman"), a kind of hominid which appeared in the grasslands of east Africa around 1.9 million years ago. The* Homo ergaster *species was strong and athletic and may have been the earliest hunters.* Homo erectus, *or "upright man," was a descendant of the African "workman." This map above shows the routes that might have been taken by the migrating hominids as traced out by the various fossil finds.*

Homo Species in Asia

One of the more developed species of the *Homo* group was *Homo erectus*. The first *Homo erectus* to have been discovered, the so-called "Java man", lived on an Indonesian island 1.8 million years ago. Similar fossils have also been found in China. The so-called "Peking man" was found near Beijing, in China, where hominid groups were living in caves. These fossil discoveries show how *Homo erectus* migrated and suggest that this species must have been able to adapt to different environments.

Fire

We know that Asian *Homo erectus* mastered the use of fire. This new skill brought enormous benefits. As well as being used for cooking and providing warmth and light, fire offered protection by frightening off animals. It could also be used for hardening stone and wooden tools. Smoke holes would have been built above the simple hearth in early shelters.

The skull of Java man, with a low forehead and thick brow-ridge, was found along the banks of the River Solo in Java.

Peopling the Rest of the Globe

Almost 2 million years after the first hominid migration, groups of modern humans migrated from Africa and gradually spread across the globe. They eventually reached Australia from Southeast Asia, arriving around 60,000 years ago. Other hunting groups migrated north and followed animal herds across what is now the Bering Strait to North America, about 18,000 years ago.

The first humans arrived in North America by crossing a land bridge from Asia. Hunter-gatherers followed ice-free corridors and river valleys (such as this one in present-day Alaska), as they slowly moved across the Arctic plain.

Homo erectus people in China around a fire in their cave shelter. They gathered wild fruit and acquired meat, an important part of their diet, by scavenging and hunting.

DATING HOMINID FOSSIL FINDS

7 million years ago
Sahelanthropus tchadensis *"Toumaï" skull in Chad.*

6 million years ago
Orrorin tugenensis *in Kenya.*

4.4 million years ago
Ardipithecus ramidus *"ground ape" in Ethiopia.*

3.2 million years ago
Australopithecus afarensis *"Lucy" skeleton in Ethiopia.*

2.5 million years ago
Paranthropus robust*us hominids.*

2.4 million years ago
Homo rudolfensis, *the first Homo species.*

1.9 million years ago
Homo habilis *makes simple stone tools.*
Homo ergaster *"workman," probably the earliest hunters.*

1.8 million years ago
Homo erectus *"Java man" lives in Indonesia.*

1.75 million years ago
Paranthropus boisei, *nicknamed "Zinj" or "Nutcracker man," in Tanzania and Kenya.*

1.6 million years ago
Homo ergaster *"Nariokotome/Turkana boy" lives in Kenya.*

800,000 years ago
Homo antecessor *lives in Europe.*

500,000 years ago
Homo erectus *"Peking man" living in caves in China.*

400,000 years ago
Homo heidelbergensis *lives in Europe.*

18,000 years ago
Homo floresiensis *was still alive on the Indonesian island of Flores, according to findings announced in 2004.*

THE FIRST STONE TOOLS

The earliest stone tools are called "Oldowan," from the site at Olduvai Gorge, in Tanzania, where they were first found. They were made up to 1.9 million years ago by Homo habilis. *They included round hammerstones, which were used to strike sharp flakes from cobble cores. Some of the chipped cobbles may have been used as tools, but the most important parts were probably the stone flakes, which made hand-held knives and scrapers. Later "Acheulean" hand axes and other tools (made by* Homo ergaster *and* Homo erectus *from about 1.5 million years ago) were named after a prehistoric site at Saint-Acheul, in northern France.*

This hand axe has two cutting edges leading to a point. These teardrop-shaped tools were made by some of our human ancestors from about 1.5 million years ago.

Fossilized antelope bone found at Olduvai Gorge. The bones of zebras, pigs, monkeys, and many other animals have also been found there, along with the stone tools that were used to cut meat from them.

Tools and Shelter

Hominids made their first tools from stone, and the oldest examples found were made up to 2.5 million years ago. These were probably used to smash open bones and extract marrow, as well as to cut meat from scavenged animals. More sophisticated hand axes and blades were useful to later hunters. Cutting and scraping tools may also have been used to shape wood and help in constructing the earliest shelters. These were simple structures, and the use of controlled fire made them warmer and safer. Tool-making, foraging, hunting, shelter-building, and fire-making must have helped bring groups of hominids closer together.

This is how a hut may have looked at Terra Amata, a prehistoric campsite in France. The bent wooden branches were held in place by rows of stones. Some huts were up to 24 feet (7.5 m) across.

Toolmakers

The early *Homo* species had larger brains than the earlier *Australopithecus* species. This enabled *Homo habilis, or* "handy man," to work out how to make effective tools. They could then butcher large carcasses; these early human-like creatures may have eaten meat regularly, scavenging rather than hunting. They probably made the tools on the spot. Later *Homo erectus* made more sophisticated tools, including hand axes with rounded grips, and may have taken them with them when they moved on.

Homo heidelbergensis *("Heidelberg man," named after a site in Germany), was an early European hominid. This skull found in Greece dates from about 450,000 years ago.*

Early Shelters

The first shelters were probably overhanging rocks and wide cave entrances. *Homo habilis* may have built camps of simple thorn-bush huts, and we know that *Homo erectus* were living in caves 500,000 years ago. About 100,000 years later, *Homo heidelbergensis* groups were building beach camps beside the Mediterranean Sea. We know this because of remains found at Terra Amata, near Nice, where large oval-shaped huts were built.

Small groups of early humans probably sheltered together in caves.

TOOL FINDS IN AFRICA, EUROPE, AND ASIA

Spread of Tool Technology

Many scientists were surprised to discover more primitive Oldowan stone tools in China and Indonesia when more sophisticated Acheulean tools had already appeared in Africa. This evidence suggests that hominids began migrating to Asia, taking Oldowan tool technology with them, before the appearance of Acheulean tools in Africa. Also, the appearance of Acheulean tools in Europe and western Asia suggests that other migration waves took place after the appearance of Acheulean tools in Africa. However, the reason why Acheulean tools never reached east Asia (past the boundary line shown on this map) is still a mystery.

Neanderthals and *Homo Sapiens*

The Neanderthals (or *Homo neanderthalensis*), emerged in Europe long before the modern humans who make up the species called *Homo sapiens* (meaning "wise man"). The two species were close relatives, though Neanderthals were shorter and stockier—well suited to a harsh ice-age existence. Nevertheless, around 27,000 years ago *Homo sapiens*—our direct ancestors—were left as the only hominid species on Earth. This probably happened as "wise" groups took over Neanderthal territories and competed with them for food and shelter. *Homo sapiens* numbers increased and *Homo neanderthalensis* became extinct.

Neanderthals

The Neanderthals were strong, stocky individuals. They had to be to survive the severely cold winters of ice-age Europe, which they did for more than 170,000 years. They hunted large animals, as well as scavenging meat and gathering plant foods. They were skillful makers of stone tools, which they used to scrape and prepare animal hides. They probably lived in small groups of up to 12 adults, moving around in search of food and sheltering in cave entrances and beneath overhanging rocks.

This bone tool, found in a French cave, was probably made and used by Neanderthals, who also appear to have made pendants and other ornaments.

Cro-Magnons

The early *Homo sapiens* who lived in Europe from about 40,000 years ago are known as Cro-Magnons, named after a site in France (see page 29). They were skilled hunters, tool-makers and artists, famous today for their cave paintings (see page 30). Cro-Magnons discovered how to start a fire by striking flint to produce sparks. They used bone needles to sew animal skins together for clothes and containers.

NEANDERTHAL AND *HOMO SAPIENS* SITES

Close Contact

Neanderthals and Homo sapiens *lived at the same time in Europe for a period of 16,000 years, and probably for longer in southwest Asia. Some groups probably occupied the same regions, in which case there would have been contact between the two species. Communication would have been difficult though, since experts believe that Cro-Magnons had a more evolved use of language than their Neanderthal neighbors.*

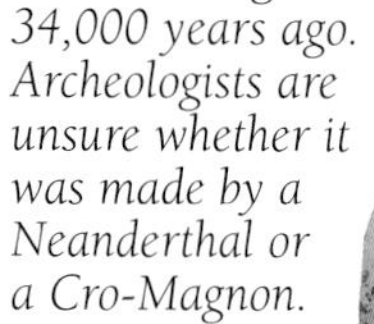

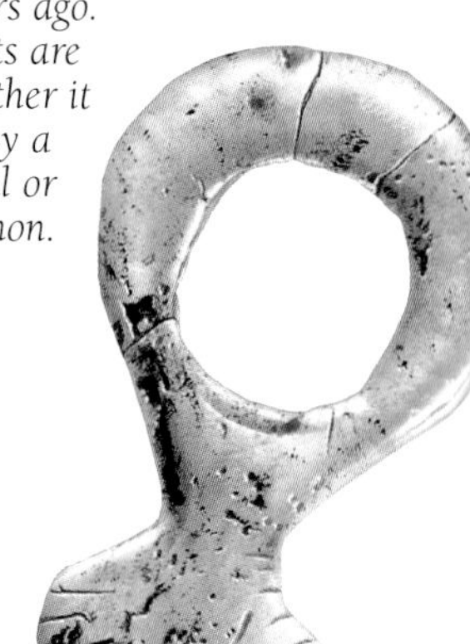

Bone pendant from a Neanderthal and Cro-Magnon site, made about 34,000 years ago. Archeologists are unsure whether it was made by a Neanderthal or a Cro-Magnon.

To withstand the cold, Neanderthals wore skins and furs. They put sharp stone points on their wooden spears.

This Cro-Magnon child's handprint was made by spraying pigment around the hand from the artist's mouth.

This child's skeleton, which is 24,500 years old, seems to have both Neanderthal and Homo sapiens features. Some scientists believe this is evidence that the two species interbred.

NEANDERTHALS VS. *HOMO SAPIENS*

The Neanderthals and early Homo sapiens, *or Cro-Magnon, appeared on Earth during the Pleistocene epoch of Earth's history (see page 5). During this epoch more than 30 percent of the Earth's surface was covered by ice.*

Dates:
Neanderthals inhabited much of Europe and the Mediterranean about 200,000–27,000 years ago. Homo sapiens *originated in Africa about 160,000–130,000 years ago.* Homo sapiens *migrated from Africa about 100,000 years ago and reached Australia about 60,000 years ago and North America about 18,000 years ago.*

Names:
The term "Neanderthalensis" comes from Neander Valley, near Düsseldorf, in Germany, where fossils of this hominid species were first found, in 1856. The term "Cro-Magnon" comes from a rock shelter near Les Eyzies, in the Dordogne region of France, where skeletons of early modern Europeans (belonging to Homo sapiens*) were found, in 1868.*

Characteristics:
Compared to Neanderthals, early Homo sapiens *were taller and more slender-boned and had a less sloping forehead, much less pronounced brow ridges, and a more pronounced chin.*

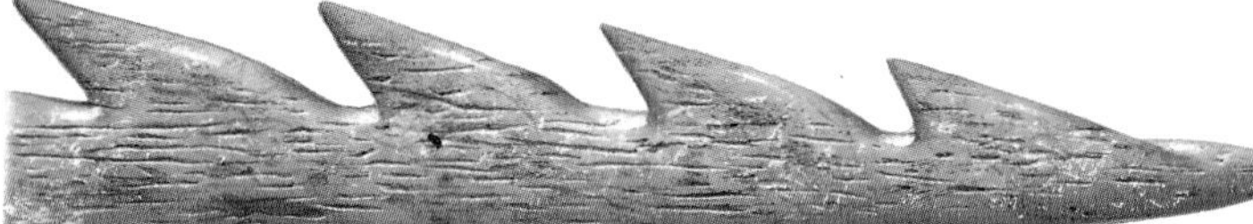

Barbed bone or antler hooks and harpoons made fishing more efficient.

Hunters and Gatherers

Prehistoric people lived as hunters and gatherers. The earliest hominids probably lived mainly on plant foods, adding meat to their diet when they happened to come across a dead animal. Later humans developed tools and worked together to improve their hunting skills. All hunter-gatherers were continually on the move, as they followed their prey and looked for new food sources. They generally stayed together in small groups, resting in rock overhangs, caves, or other simple shelters until it was time to move on again. Within each group, men were the hunters, while women concentrated on gathering plant foods.

This strange fish-like sculpture comes from a prehistoric site beside the River Danube in Serbia. Remains show that fish from the Danube played an important part in hunter-gatherers' diet.

Fishing

Early modern humans used spears and clubs to catch river fish which were a good source of high-protein food. Hunter-gatherers would have followed rivers and streams so as to be near a source of fresh water. Near the coast, they may have used the same approach and also collected shellfish. Around 25,000 years ago, fishermen were using the fish gorge, a baited toggle attached to a line that wedged in a fish's jaws. This was followed by the fish hook and barbed harpoon.

A Cro-Magnon man stands in a river and spears fish with a barbed harpoon. Later, fishermen learned to make wooden fences so that the trapped fish were easier to spear.

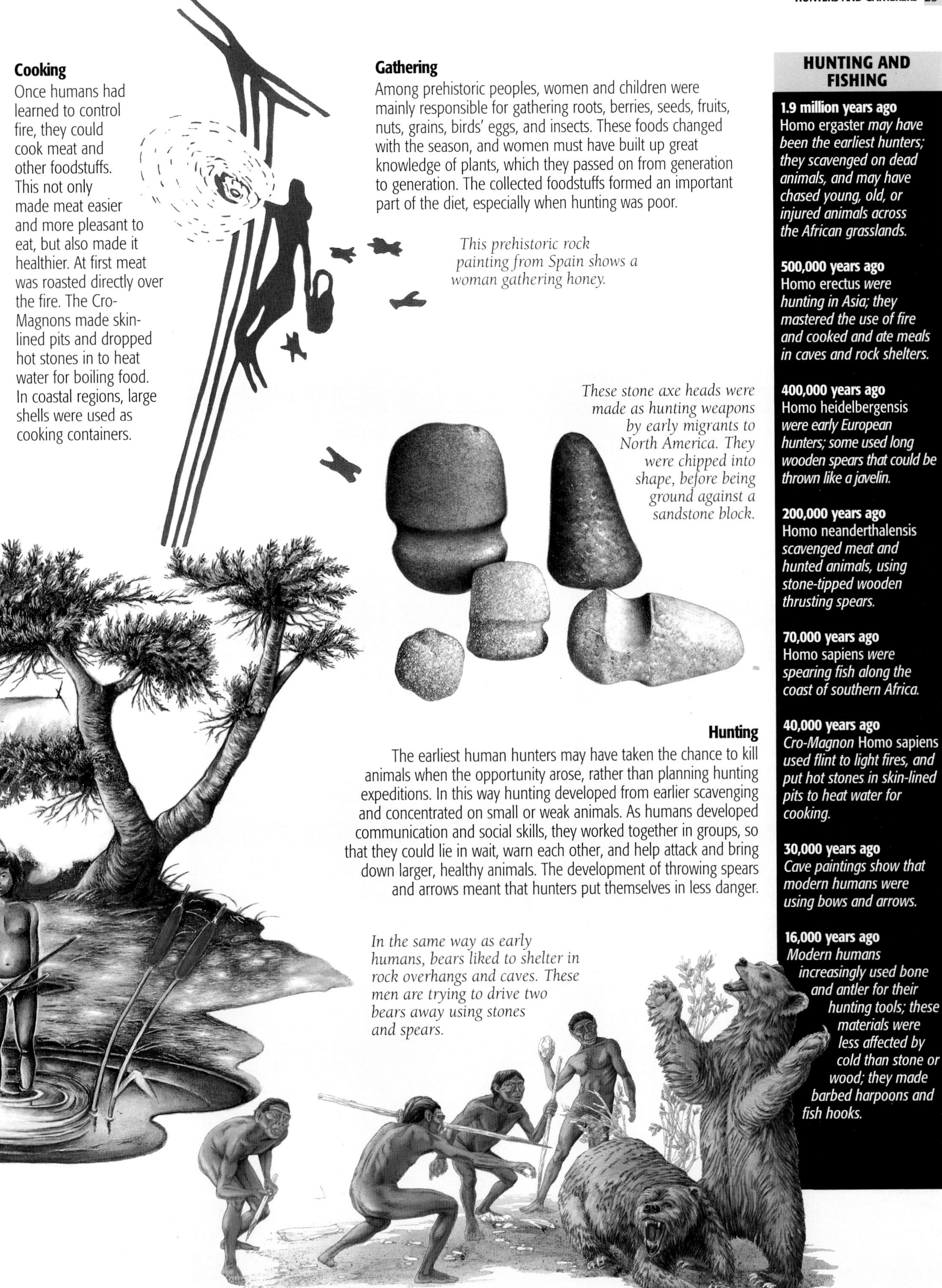

Cooking

Once humans had learned to control fire, they could cook meat and other foodstuffs. This not only made meat easier and more pleasant to eat, but also made it healthier. At first meat was roasted directly over the fire. The Cro-Magnons made skin-lined pits and dropped hot stones in to heat water for boiling food. In coastal regions, large shells were used as cooking containers.

Gathering

Among prehistoric peoples, women and children were mainly responsible for gathering roots, berries, seeds, fruits, nuts, grains, birds' eggs, and insects. These foods changed with the season, and women must have built up great knowledge of plants, which they passed on from generation to generation. The collected foodstuffs formed an important part of the diet, especially when hunting was poor.

This prehistoric rock painting from Spain shows a woman gathering honey.

These stone axe heads were made as hunting weapons by early migrants to North America. They were chipped into shape, before being ground against a sandstone block.

Hunting

The earliest human hunters may have taken the chance to kill animals when the opportunity arose, rather than planning hunting expeditions. In this way hunting developed from earlier scavenging and concentrated on small or weak animals. As humans developed communication and social skills, they worked together in groups, so that they could lie in wait, warn each other, and help attack and bring down larger, healthy animals. The development of throwing spears and arrows meant that hunters put themselves in less danger.

In the same way as early humans, bears liked to shelter in rock overhangs and caves. These men are trying to drive two bears away using stones and spears.

HUNTING AND FISHING

1.9 million years ago
Homo ergaster *may have been the earliest hunters; they scavenged on dead animals, and may have chased young, old, or injured animals across the African grasslands.*

500,000 years ago
Homo erectus *were hunting in Asia; they mastered the use of fire and cooked and ate meals in caves and rock shelters.*

400,000 years ago
Homo heidelbergensis *were early European hunters; some used long wooden spears that could be thrown like a javelin.*

200,000 years ago
Homo neanderthalensis *scavenged meat and hunted animals, using stone-tipped wooden thrusting spears.*

70,000 years ago
Homo sapiens *were spearing fish along the coast of southern Africa.*

40,000 years ago
Cro-Magnon Homo sapiens *used flint to light fires, and put hot stones in skin-lined pits to heat water for cooking.*

30,000 years ago
Cave paintings show that modern humans were using bows and arrows.

16,000 years ago
Modern humans increasingly used bone and antler for their hunting tools; these materials were less affected by cold than stone or wood; they made barbed harpoons and fish hooks.

Religion and Rituals

Prehistoric people probably believed that spirits dwelled in the natural phenomena essential to life, such as sunshine and rain. Through magical rituals, prehistoric people thought that they could control natural events by pleasing these spirits. Some rituals, for example, would have been performed to ensure the fertility of the Earth, which was vital for a plentiful food supply. Although it is difficult to clearly define religion before the invention of writing, archeological finds, such as burial sites, representations of deities, and remains of temples or altars are evidence of early religious expression. We can only guess at the meaning and ritual use of these finds.

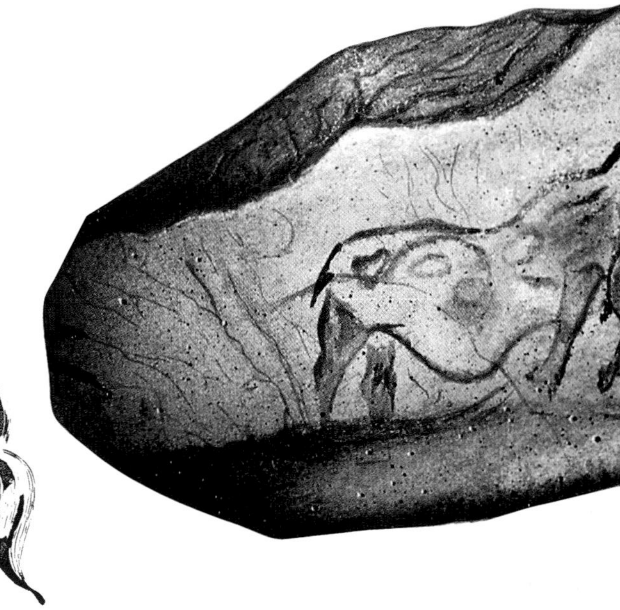

Figure of a shaman, perhaps performing a hunting dance, shown as a mix of different animals from a cave in France.

Ceremonial Sites

The world's earliest stone monuments, or megaliths, were probably raised for ritual function (see pages 34–35). Among the earliest examples are the great stone temples on the islands of Malta, situated south of Sicily in the Mediterranean Sea. It is believed that these temples were built for fertility rituals. Altars (possibly used for animal sacrifice), decorative reliefs, and statuettes of deities and "priests" were found at these sites.

Hağar Qim, the best preserved of the Maltese temples, seen from above. The rounded divisions give the structure an organic form.

Detail of a cave painting from Lascaux, France, showing prehistoric cattle and other, possibly, mythical, beasts.

Fertility Cults

Some archeological evidence has led experts to believe that dances may have been performed to promote the fertility of the animals on which people depended for their food supply. Footprints, thought to be of dancers, were found in a cave in France around a small mound decorated with a male and female bison. The dancers may have thought that this ritual had a magical effect, increasing the number of bison available for the hunt.

The clay bison in the cave at Tuc d'Audobert, France, were modeled in relief on a projecting stone about 14,000 years ago.

Art and Ritual

Other possible evidence of the celebration of rituals and ceremonies is found in cave paintings (see page 30). Some caves were perhaps seen as sanctuaries, since they were not used as living quarters. Paintings of animals and hunting scenes may have been made to exert some kind of control, through ritual and magic, over the animals and the hunt. Magicians, or shamen, who were believed to be in touch with the spirits, may have led the rituals.

The famous 30,000 year-old Venus of Willendorf (below). *Many female figures were carved in limestone, showing exaggerated features.*

VENUS FIGURINES IN EUROPE

Mother Goddesses

This map shows sites in Europe where figurines commonly known as "Venuses" have been found. Some experts have suggested that these figurines represented the life-giving forces of nature, fertility, and growth. People may have believed that a kind of mother-goddess reigned over the fruitfulness of all life on Earth and that these figurines possessed magical fertility powers.

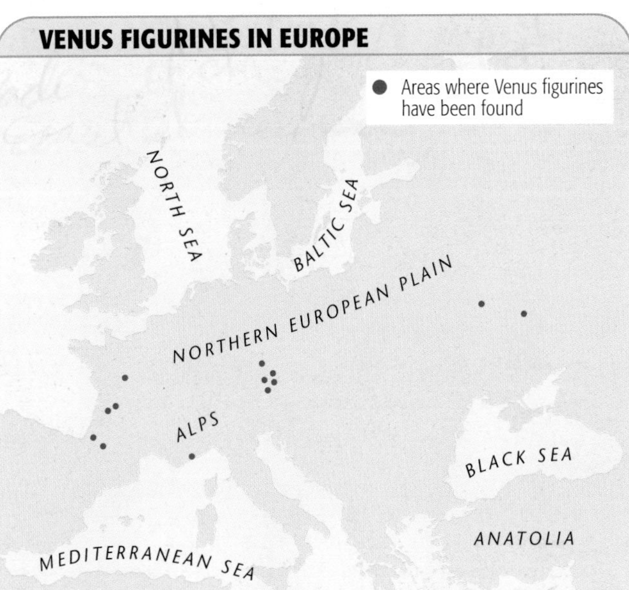

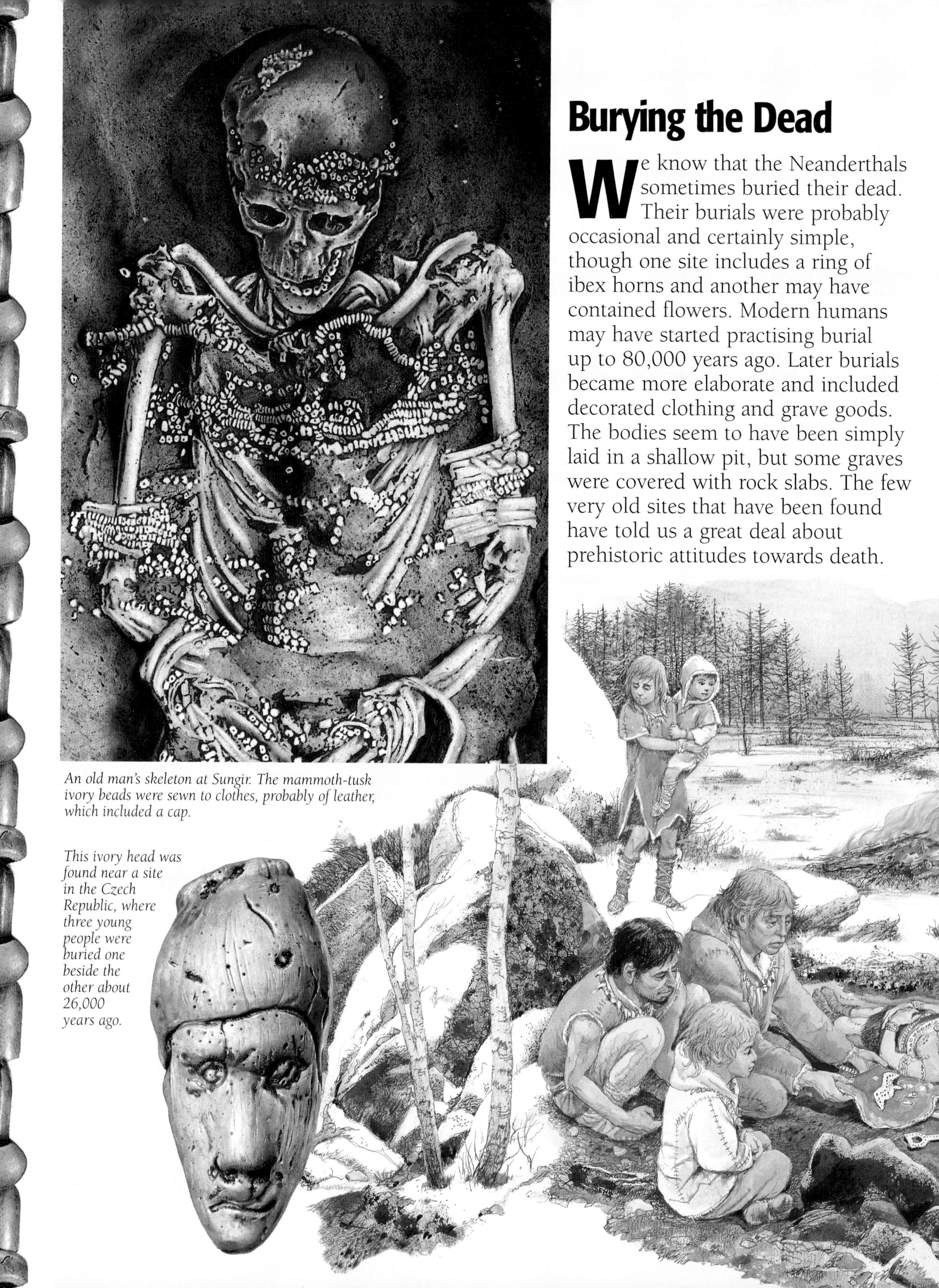

Burying the Dead

We know that the Neanderthals sometimes buried their dead. Their burials were probably occasional and certainly simple, though one site includes a ring of ibex horns and another may have contained flowers. Modern humans may have started practising burial up to 80,000 years ago. Later burials became more elaborate and included decorated clothing and grave goods. The bodies seem to have been simply laid in a shallow pit, but some graves were covered with rock slabs. The few very old sites that have been found have told us a great deal about prehistoric attitudes towards death.

An old man's skeleton at Sungir. The mammoth-tusk ivory beads were sewn to clothes, probably of leather, which included a cap.

This ivory head was found near a site in the Czech Republic, where three young people were buried one beside the other about 26,000 years ago.

Burials

The little evidence that archeologists have found shows that more elaborate burial began about 35,000 years ago. A burial site discovered at Sungir, near the modern city of Vladimir in Russia, dates from 28,000 years ago. The bodies had been put in shallow graves that had been dug in the frozen earth. They were dressed in clothing sewn with thousands of ivory beads.

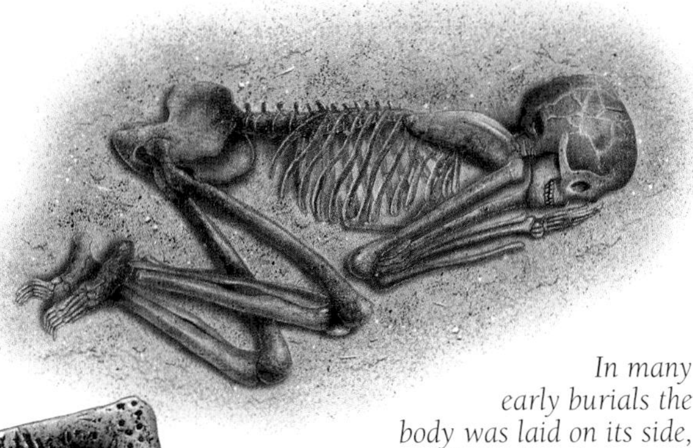

In many early burials the body was laid on its side, with the legs drawn up.

SOME EARLY BURIAL SITES

c. 80,000–60,000 years ago:
Shanidar cave, Zagros Mountains, Iraq; discovered 1951; Neanderthal burial site with seven adults and one child. One grave was rich in pollen, suggesting that the burial may have been on a bed of flowers.

c. 70,000 years ago:
Teshik-Tash, Uzbekistan; discovered 1938; Neanderthal site, with an adolescent seemingly buried within a ring of ibex horns.

c. 32,000–30,000 years ago:
Cro-Magnon, Les Eyzies, France; discovered 1868; 5 modern human (since called Cro-Magnon) skeletons–three adult males, one adult female, and one infant; burial with body adornments.

c. 30,000–25,000 years ago:
Predmosti, Czech Republic; discovered 1894, destroyed 1945 (in World War II); remains of ten modern human children and eight adults in a large oval pit beneath stone slabs and mammoth bones with ornaments and grave goods.

c. 28,000 years ago:
Sungir, Russia; discovered 1956; remains of five modern humans, including a 60-year-old man, an 8-year-old girl, and a 13-year-old boy buried together in a head-to-head position; the man's body was adorned with 2,900 beads, as well as Arctic fox teeth; the boy was covered with 4,900 beads, and the girl had 5,200 (each single bead may have taken up to an hour to make!); next to the boy were two straightened mammoth tusks.

Grave Goods

The individuals found at Sungir were buried with different kinds of grave goods. These included carved pendants, bracelets, and shell necklaces. While ornaments, tools, and weapons have been found at some Cro-Magnon burial sites, such as this one, others are much simpler. This indicates a difference in importance and status between individuals, suggesting a social hierarchy of leaders and followers.

Ivory cloak pin, found on the remains of a Sungir boy.

A small pendant of a horse found at Sungir. It was carved out of mammoth-tusk ivory, and its cut outline is considered unusual for such an early time.

Belief in an Afterlife

Experts believe that prehistoric people would only have buried their dead with grave goods if they thought the items would be useful to the deceased. This means that Cro-Magnons must have believed in some form of afterlife. Burying their dead must have made them think about a world beyond their everyday environment. Like a lot of prehistoric art, grave goods may be seen as evidence of early religious expression.

This strange, ghost-shaped figurine, carved in mammoth ivory, was found at Mezhirich, in Ukraine. This was the site of a 15,000-year-old campsite of huts made of mammoth bones.

The bodies at Sungir were laid on their backs, with their arms folded across their stomachs.

One of the many horses painted on the walls and ceilings at Lascaux. The artist succeeded in achieving a sense of depth and movement.

Prehistoric Art

Cave paintings are the most famous form of art created by prehistoric humans, and some date back more than 30,000 years. Sculptures and decorative items have been found that are even older, including a recent find that takes abstract art back 70,000 years. Many theories have been put forward as to the purpose of such works of art, including ideas about magic, religion, and hunting rituals. Experts agree that these works may have had a symbolic meaning for their creators, and they certainly represented a way for them to express their feelings and beliefs.

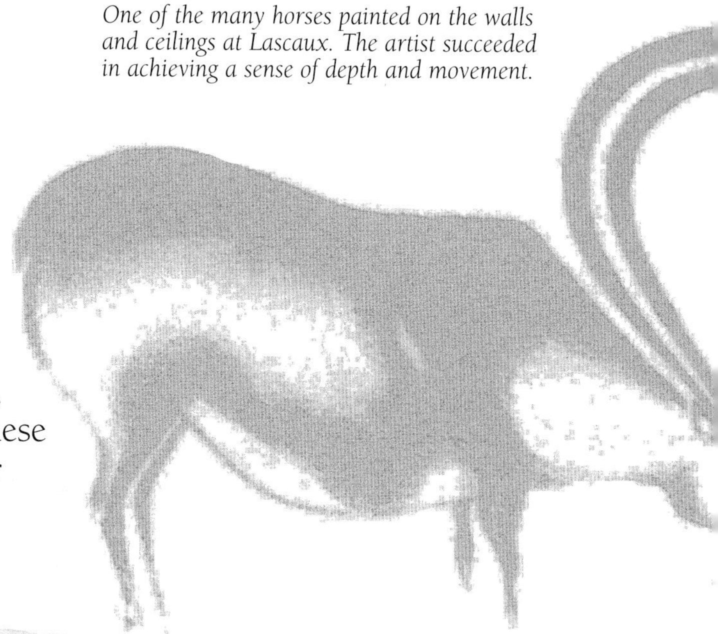

This delicate painting of reindeer was created in Font de Gaume cave, in southwest France, about 14,000 years ago.

Cave Painting

Using stone lamps filled with animal fat to light the pitch-dark caves, prehistoric artists depicted mainly animals–horses, bison, ibex, aurochs (long-horned wild oxen, now extinct), deer, and mammoths. At Lascaux there are also dots and geometric shapes, and one single representation of a man. The cave surfaces were easy to reach; the ceilings would have been just a few feet from the floor. Today most cave art sites have been dug out to create higher ceilings, making them more easily accessible to visitors.

Detail of the Carnarvon Gorge rock painting site in Australia, where stencil designs were made on sandstone cliffs.

Jewelry

Necklaces, bracelets, and other items were made from beads, animal teeth, and shells. Beads were made of ivory (mainly from mammoth tusks), bone, antler, and stone pebbles. The teeth were canines of fox, but wolf, bear, and lion teeth were also used. Seashells from the Atlantic and Mediterranean coasts have been found in French and Spanish caves. All these items were pierced with pointed tools, before being strung together and attached to clothing or worn separately.

Ivory statue of a human body with a lion's head from Germany, carved more than 30,000 years ago.

Portable Art

Artists sculpted shapes and figurines from stone, and later from ivory, bone, and antler. The oldest examples of these include simple carvings of animals. Other, later, examples of portable art include the so-called Venus figurines (see page 27). As carving techniques became more sophisticated, simple incisions and dots gave way to more realistic representations. Artistic carvings were also added to some weapons and tools, such as spear-throwers.

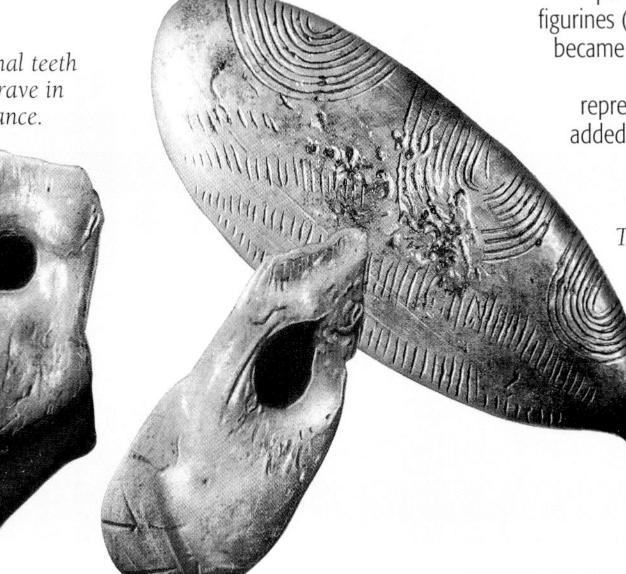

Pierced animal teeth found in a grave in southern France.

This piece of iron ore was shaped and carved with geometric patterns more than 70,000 years ago. It was found in a cave in South Africa and may be the world's oldest example of abstract art.

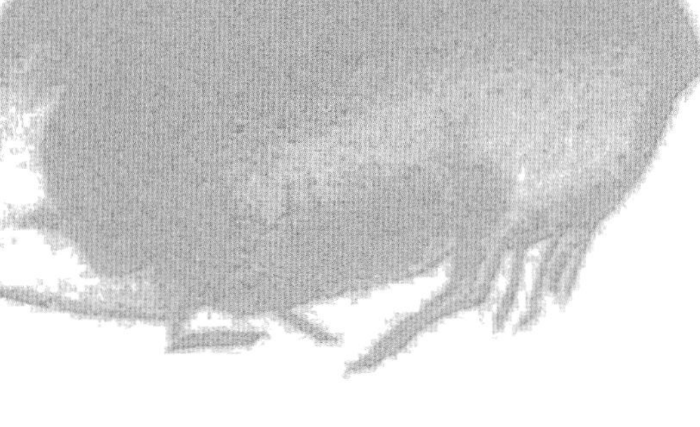

Use of Color

Artists worked with the surfaces as they found them. They chose smooth surfaces for painting, using contours to add depth. Their main colors were black, obtained from manganese or charcoal, and red, which came from ochre (a form of iron oxide mixed with clay and sand that produced a range of colors from deep red to light yellow). The minerals were scraped and crushed into powder form and then mixed with water.

PREHISTORIC PAINTING

Africa:
Twyfelfontein, Damaraland, Namibia; painted c. 25,000 years ago; images of animals painted in red and black pigment.

Australia:
Carnarvon Gorge, Queensland; 646 stencils of hands, forearms, boomerangs, and axes were created by blowing a spray of pigment mixed with water from the mouth over objects held up against the surface.

Europe:
Altamira, Spain; decorated c. 14,000 years ago; S-shaped cave about 885 feet (270 m) long; main galleries decorated with engravings and black outline paintings of bison, horses, aurochs, ibexes, deer, and boar; also geometric signs.

Chauvet, France; decorated c. 32,000 years ago; mainly paintings of rhinoceroses, lions, mammoths, horses, bison, bears, reindeer, aurochs, ibexes, stags, a red panther, and an engraved owl; no human images, but one composite being, half-man, half-bison.

Lascaux, France; decorated c. 17,000 years ago; seven chambers, with 600 paintings and 1500 engravings.

A selection of minerals used by prehistoric painters. White clay or chalk was added in later times. The pigments were applied with fingers, pads of vegetable fibers, or simple brushes made of twigs or fur.

HUMAN PREHISTORY

Human prehistory is divided by stages in development. Different parts of the world reached these stages at different times, so dates of these periods vary from region to region. The first stage is called the Paleolithic age. Experts divide the early Paleolithic age in Europe (40,000–10,000 years ago) into the following cultures or periods which are named after prehistoric sites in southern France:

Aurignacian
c. 40,000–28,000 years ago, named after Aurignac, a site discovered in 1860. During this time advanced tools and the first bone spear points were used along with other tools made of stone.

Gravettian
c. 28,000–22,000 years ago, named after La Gravette cave. Neanderthals used backed blades, the first eyed bone needles, and ivory beads as ornaments. They also decorated spear-throwers and baked-clay figurines.

Solutrean
c. 22,000–18,000 years ago, named after Solutré, a horse-hunting site discovered in 1867. Elegant tools, which were sometimes improved by heating and cooling flint, were used.

Magdalenian
c. 18,000–10,000 years ago, named after La Madeleine, a site discovered in 1863. During this time there was an increased use of very small flaked stones and barbed harpoon points made of bone and antler. Bows and arrows appeared. The Magdalenian is also known as the "golden age" of Ice Age art.

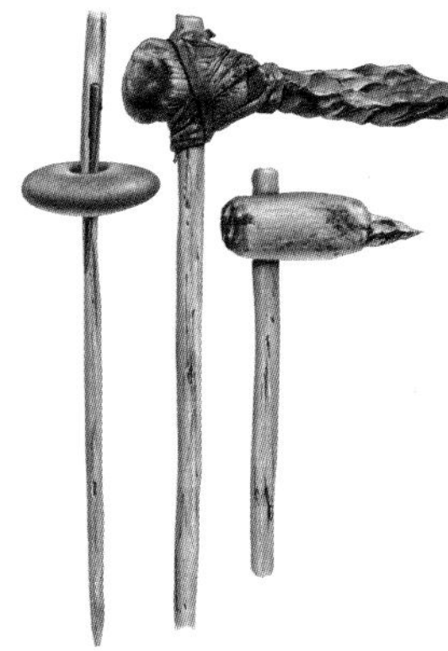

Composite tools: (left) a simple tool for digging up roots was made from a stick weighted with a smooth pierced pebble; (center) the stone head was fixed firmly into a shaped piece of horn, which was attached to a wooden handle with a leather strap; (right) this smaller tool has a sharp flint blade at the end of a wooden axehead.

This family of reindeer-hunters is busy making tools near their campfire. Generations of children learned tool-making skills by watching their parents.

Prehistoric Technology

Early technology revolved around the making of tools which made it possible for prehistoric people to hunt animals, dig up roots, and make shelters. During the last period of the Paleolithic, or Old Stone Age, the human hunter-gatherers' toolkit became more intricate, as individuals spent more time crafting a range of stone blades and points. These were used to carve bone and wood, which were used in large composite tools (see left), as well as for small, delicate needles. Towards the end of the period, new technologies were discovered, as people started to shape baked clay into pots and hammer copper into figurines.

Using Stone, Flint, and Wood

Many stone tools were fashioned from flint, a hard rock that ranges in color from brown to dark grey and black, which can be chipped into flakes more easily than other kinds of rock. As toolmakers became more skillful, they made smaller, more delicate tools from flakes of flint. These were very useful for shaping bone, antler, and wood. Points of bone or antler were used to produce even more razor-sharp slices of flint. Shaped wood was used to make handles for axes and spears. The handle gave the user a firmer grip and greater leverage.

Another late Palaeolithic invention was the arrow. This painting from a rock shelter in Spain shows a group of archers shooting their arrows at a herd of deer.

Making Clothing

Neanderthals and early modern humans probably wore clothing made of animal hides tied together with thongs or leather strips. The introduction of sharper tools and needles with eyes made them easier to cut and shape. Plant fibers were used much later, and the earliest known textiles are the linens found at Çatal Hüyük (see page 38), dating from about 6500 BCE.

With sharper flint tools animals could be easily skinned.

The Invention of Pottery

The first pots were made in Japan about 12,500 years ago. Potters pressed coils or lumps of wet clay together into the shape of a vessel, smoothed the sides and then baked it in an open fire. This fired the clay so that it was hard and dry. The early Japanese pot-making culture is known as Jomon.

Cone-shaped Japanese cooking pot, with typical rope-pattern markings, from around 6000 BCE.

Early Use of Metal

The first metal to be used was copper, which was found as nuggets in rocks. A soft metal, it could be beaten into shape for use in tools and ornaments. Copper was probably first used in the region of Mesopotamia about 10,000 years ago. Early metalworkers soon learned to heat the metal, so that it could be hammered without becoming brittle. Some time after 5000 BCE, people discovered how to extract metal from its ore by smelting.

These small copper models of long-horned oxen were made about 6,000 years ago in eastern Europe.

STONE MONUMENTS

c. 4500–2500 BCE
Megalithic monuments are built in the Carnac region of Brittany, France.

c. 3500–2500 BCE
Megalithic temples are built at Tarxien, Malta.

c. 3200 BCE
The megalithic chamber tomb is built at Newgrange, Ireland.

c. 3100–1000 BCE
Stonehenge is built and rebuilt several times on Salisbury Plain, England.

c. 2600 BCE
Avebury stone circle is begun in England.

c. 1500 BCE
San Agustín culture begins to develop in Colombia.

c. 1200–900 BCE
Olmec ceremonial center of San Lorenzo flourishes.

c. 600–100 BCE
The mound-building Adena culture flourishes around Ohio, USA.

At Stonehenge, prehistoric builders probably used ropes to pull the huge stones upright. They may have used scaffolding to put the lintel stones on top.

Monument Building

Around 6,500 years ago, people started building megaliths, or large stone monuments. Some of the earliest examples, in western Europe, served as communal tombs. At other sites huge stones were placed in rows and circles; we do not know precisely what took place there. People may have used these structures to celebrate harvests and the fertility of the land, as well as to note the changing of the seasons. At Stonehenge, for example, some stones line up with the rising and setting Sun on certain days of the year. Megalithic monuments were also built in other parts of the world, as tombs and important features of ceremonial centers.

European Megaliths

There are a number of prehistoric sites throughout Europe where megaliths arranged in circles still stand. At Stonehenge, on Salisbury Plain in west England, there was originally a circle of massive upright stones 98 feet (30 m) wide, with lintel stones on top. There were further horseshoe shapes inside the circle, which was surrounded by a bank and ditch. The largest stone is 30 feet (9 m) long and weighs about 40 tons. At other sites, such as Carnac in France, there are rows of single upright megalithic stones known as menhirs.

These beads, made of variscite stone, were found at a megalithic site in Brittany, France.

A row of Easter Island statues, or moai. The statues were toppled in the 18th century, but many have been re-erected.

Giant Heads

The Olmecs lived in the coastal regions of the Mexican Gulf. They are most famous for the huge heads that they carved from stone. They transported basalt boulders from mountains 50 miles (80 km) away, before carving them into heads up to 11 feet (3.4 m) high. Seventeen giant heads have been discovered, and many experts believe that they were probably intended as portraits of chiefs or rulers.

The monolithic figure standing outside this tomb at San Agustín has feline fangs and holds a tool in each hand.

Each giant Olmec head was carved wearing a helmet-like headpiece. The largest head weighs about 50 tons.

Monumental Tombs

The prehistoric site of San Agustín in Colombia contains many imposing megalithic monuments and tombs. Monolithic figures with both human and animal traits were created to guard the dolmen tombs. Many scholars believe that these statues represent deities or priests.

Stone Statues

Easter Island, in the Pacific Ocean, is the world's remotest inhabited place. Between 1000 and 1500 CE, the island's Polynesian inhabitants carved and erected up to 1,000 stone statues. They stood on stone platforms facing inland, and the largest was over 65 feet (20 m) tall. Their purpose remains a mystery, but many experts believe that they represented revered ancestors of the islanders' community. This culture probably declined when the island no longer had enough food or timber to support the population.

The First Farmers

At the end of the last ice age, about 10,000 years ago, the Earth generally became warmer and drier and the landscape changed. In some parts of the world hunter-gatherers began planting seeds in one place and settling there. They continued to hunt for meat, but gradually domesticated animals which could also be kept near their settlements. In this way the early farmers of Mesopotamia and elsewhere controlled the supply of their food and completely changed their way of life. Since fresh water was essential to the well-being of their plants, animals, and themselves, the earliest farmers settled in great river valleys in different parts of the world.

Animals

Animals were domesticated by separating them from their wild herds. Farmers soon learned that these animals could provide milk, hides, and wool, as well as meat, and that they could also pull and carry loads. Sheep and goats were herded in Mesopotamia, gazelle in the Middle East, pigs in Anatolia (present-day Turkey) and China, cattle in North Africa and around the Aegean region, and llamas and guinea pigs in South America.

This small figurine of a dog is more than 5,000 years old. It comes from Egypt, where dogs helped with hunting and later became domestic pets. Earlier hunter-gatherers probably used wolves, the ancestors of all dogs, in the hunt.

FARMING AROUND THE WORLD

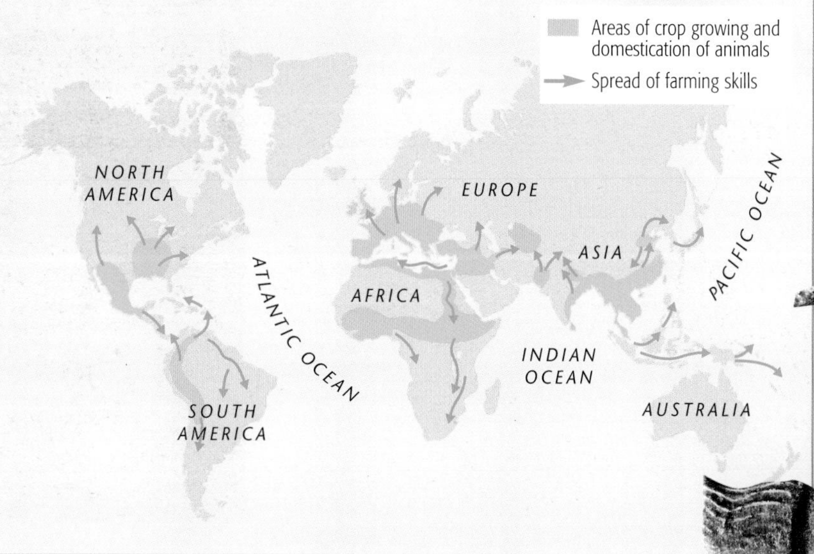

The Spread of Farming

By 6000 BCE, there were settled farmers in southwest and eastern Asia, northern Africa, and southern Europe. About 3,000 years later, farming had also developed in Central America and the Andes region of South America.

Irrigation

Early Mesopotamian farmers had to deal with floods in spring, when their fields were full of young crops, and drought conditions later in the growing season. Some time after 7000 BCE, they began building dykes and embankments to hold back the floodwaters of the Euphrates and Tigris rivers. They also dug irrigation canals and water-storage basins, so that they could use the rivers' water throughout the year.

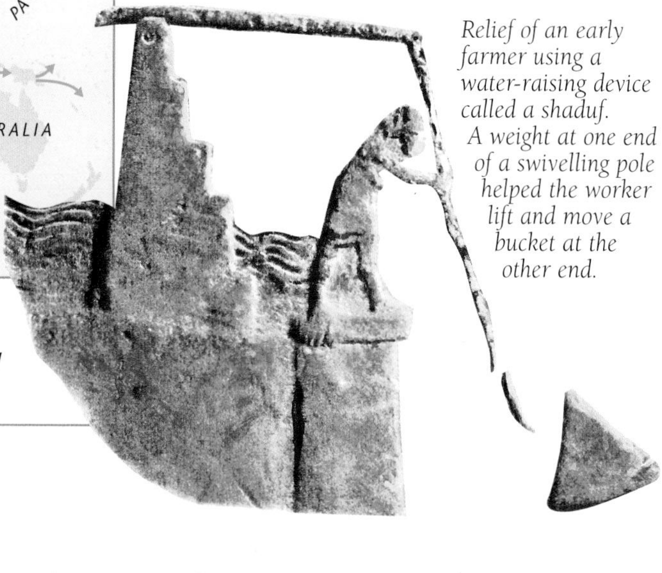

Relief of an early farmer using a water-raising device called a shaduf. A weight at one end of a swivelling pole helped the worker lift and move a bucket at the other end.

Mesopotamian farmers harvesting wheat. At harvest time all members of the family were put to work.

FARMING DEVELOPMENT

c. 10,000 BCE
Hunter-gatherers harvest wild cereals in the Middle East.

c. 8000 BCE
The first farmers in Mesopotamia.

c. 7000 BCE
Settled farmers begin irrigating their fields in southern Mesopotamia (dry farming in the north) while millet farming is under way in Yellow River Valley, northern China.

c. 6500 BCE
Rice farming in Yangzi Valley, southern China.

c.6000 BCE
Cattle herding in northern Africa; first cattle domesticated in the Middle East; farming in the Indus Valley and southern Europe.

c. 5000 BCE
Farming spreads to central Europe.

c. 4500 BCE
Farming villages develop into small towns; earliest plows used; wheat and barley in the Nile Valley; farming on the River Ganges plain.

c. 3600 BCE
Farming of maize and beans in Central America.

c. 3500 BCE
Linen produced from flax in Egypt.

c. 3000 BCE
Potatoes and quinoa in the Andes, using terraced fields.

Farming Tools

Early farmers used pointed digging sticks to prepare the ground for sowing their seeds. The first simple wooden plows were used to turn the soil in Mesopotamia around 4500 BCE, and by about 3000 BCE a bronze plowshare had been added. This made a much deeper furrow in hard ground further away from irrigated land. Wheeled carts were introduced at about the same time.

Terra-cotta model of a bullock cart, from the Indus Valley.

Early Crops

In Mesopotamia, the first farmers collected and planted the seeds of wild cereals, such as wheat and barley. At each harvest they kept the seeds of the best cereals and sowed them the following season. In this way the crops developed and improved. In northern China, around the valley of the Yellow River (Huang He) early farmers did the same with millet, and in the valley of the River Yangzi (Chang Jiang), they domesticated rice. In Central America the main crop was another cereal—maize—along with beans and squash.

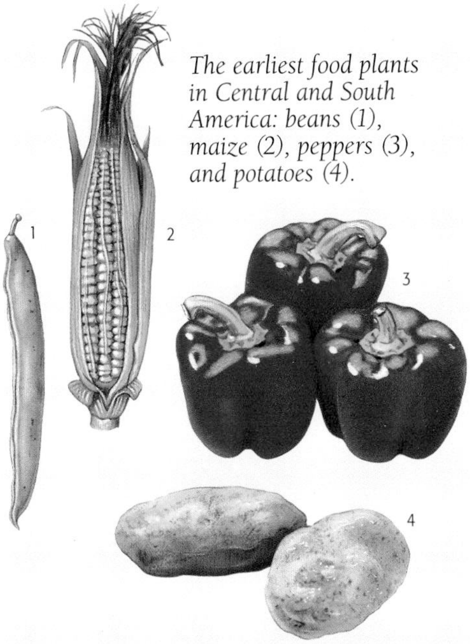

The earliest food plants in Central and South America: beans (1), maize (2), peppers (3), and potatoes (4).

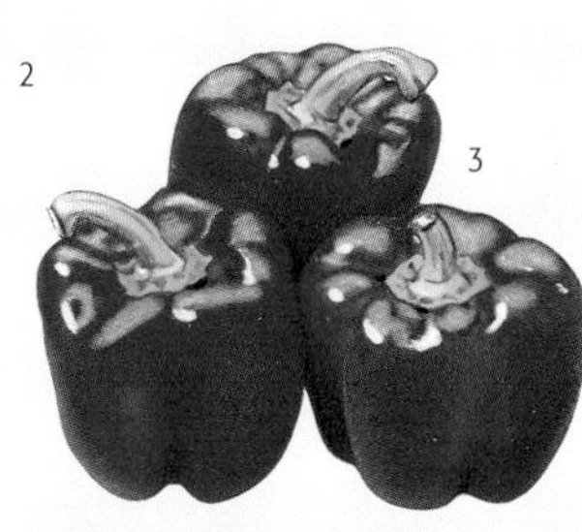

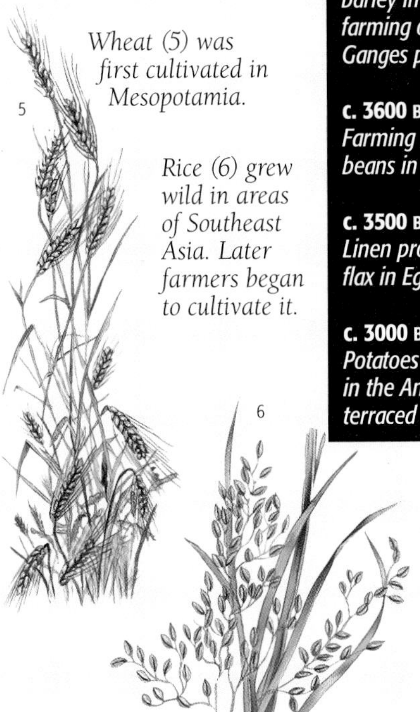

Wheat (5) was first cultivated in Mesopotamia.

Rice (6) grew wild in areas of Southeast Asia. Later farmers began to cultivate it.

Settling Down

Villages grew up near settled farmers' fields, as people started building stronger, more permanent houses. Families often shared a single dwelling, and houses were built very close together. Structures varied according to the climate and availability of building materials, from mud bricks in warm river valleys to stone slabs near cooler coasts. Good harvests and the successful storage of food meant that some people had time to do other things, such as make jewellery and pottery. Settled people began making useful items that earlier hunter-gatherers would have found too heavy and breakable.

This carved bone necklace was found at Skara Brae.

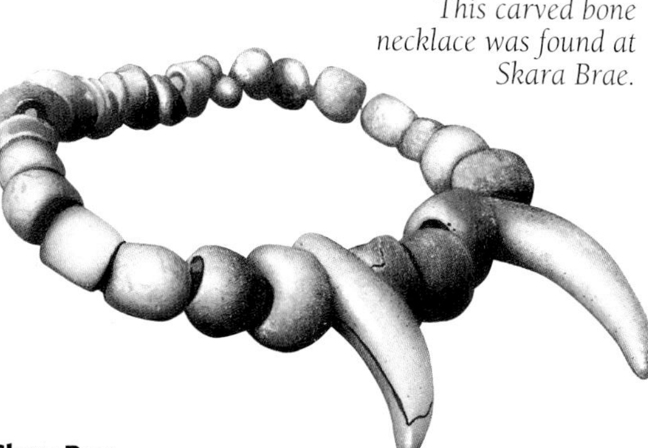

Skara Brae

The settlement of Skara Brae lay on Mainland, one of the Orkney Islands off the northeast coast of Scotland. There was good pastureland on the island but little wood, so the villagers built and furnished their houses with stone. These substantial structures kept out the cold and wet of a northern European winter, though the settlement may eventually have been abandoned because of severe storms.

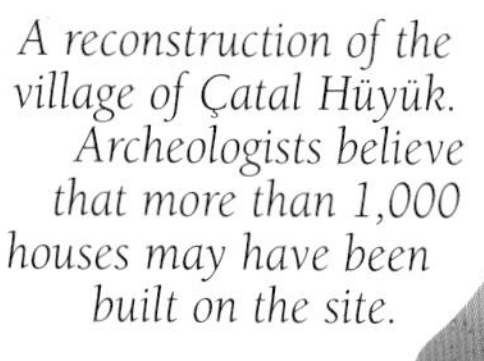

A reconstruction of the village of Çatal Hüyük. Archeologists believe that more than 1,000 houses may have been built on the site.

A reconstructed scene of everyday village life at Skara Brae. A cut-away section shows a woman tending to the hearth in a one-room stone dwelling.

Çatal Hüyük

People founded a farming village at Çatal Hüyük, in Anatolia, around 7000 BCE. They built rectangular mud-brick houses that adjoined each other. There were entrances on the flat roofs, and ladders were used to connect the different levels. All around the growing settlement, villagers grew crops of wheat, barley, lentils, and peas.

Mesopotamia

Some time after 7000 BCE, farming villages grew up beside the Euphrates and Tigris rivers. The villagers built their simple houses of sundried mud bricks, and villages began to appear further south as Mesopotamian techniques of irrigation improved. We know that some villages were surrounded by a mudbrick wall and a defensive ditch.

Villagers began to use clay pots as storage containers and cooking vessels. This Mesopotamian pottery beaker dates back to about 4000 BCE.

EARLY SETTLEMENTS AND VILLAGES

c. 8000 BCE
Settlement of Jericho near a spring, surrounded by cereal fields.

c.7000 BCE
Foundation of Çatal Hüyük, in Anatolia.

c. 6000 BCE
Farming villages established in the Mediterranean region; also in China, where pigs and dogs are kept.

c. 5500 BCE
Domed round houses of the Halaf culture, in northern Syria.

c. 5000 BCE
Ubaid culture of Mesopotamia based on irrigation farming.

c. 3400 BCE
Villages of round pit houses in the Tehuacán Valley, Mexico.

c. 3300 BCE
Walled towns appear in ancient Egypt.

c. 3100–2500 BCE
Farming and fishing village of Skara Brae in the Orkney Islands, Scotland.

c. 2800 BCE
Villages appear in the region of the River Amazon in South America.

c. 1150 BCE
Large villages in the Valley of Oaxaca, Mexico.

Africa

By about 6000 BCE nomadic peoples of the Sahara Desert were cultivating millet, and later sorghum and rice. Farming villages appeared in the Nile River valley in about 4000 BCE after wheat and barley were introduced from western Asia. Early Egyptian villages were made up of perhaps 50 people, but they soon grew to a population of around 1,000.

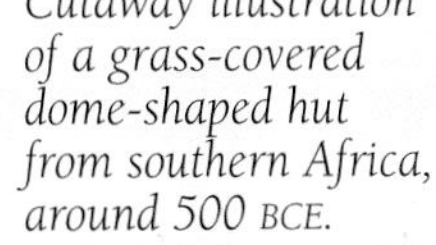

Cutaway illustration of a grass-covered dome-shaped hut from southern Africa, around 500 BCE.

Central and South America

Maize was probably being farmed in the Tehuacán Valley of Mexico by 5000 BCE, and villages of up to ten pit houses developed there. In South America, the first permanent villages grew up near the Pacific coast in present-day Peru, where cotton was being cultivated by 3500 BCE. About 1,000 years later, settlements were growing up in the river valleys leading down from the Andes Mountains to the coast.

Painted pottery figurine from the Tehuacán Valley.

Clay image of a goddess from the Hongshan culture, which developed in northern China around 4500 BCE.

South and East Asia

Early farming villages developed near the River Bolan on the Kachhi Plain, in modern Pakistan. From about 6000 BCE, villagers in this region were also building mudbrick storehouses. At around the same time, farming villages such as Banpo were appearing in northern China, near the Yellow River. There farming families lived in round huts with walls made of a mixture of mud and straw and supported by wooden posts.

The Growth of Towns

Cities developed in similar ways at different times in various parts of the world. The first large urban centers appeared in Mesopotamia. As farming populations increased, small villages grew into towns and some eventually became cities. In order to organize communities and control social living, hierarchies grew up in the cities and these led to the rule of kings. For defence against others, cities were generally walled. People living in well-organized communities were able to build temples and palaces and begin trading with other similar communities.

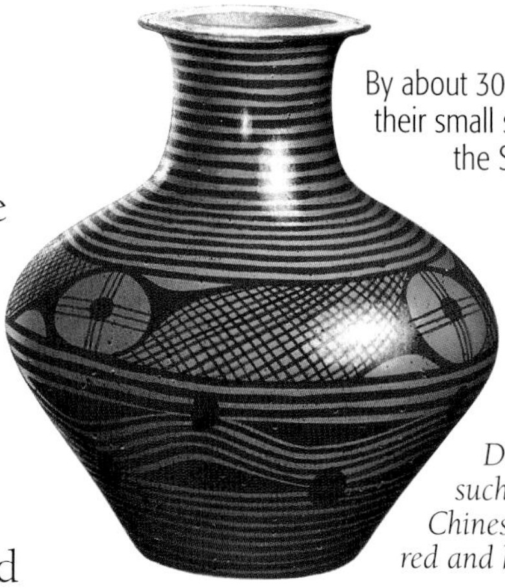

China

By about 3000 BCE Chinese villagers began to protect their small settlements with earth walls. Later, under the Shang dynasty of rulers (who began their reign soon after 1800 BCE), several cities developed and became successive capitals. Two of the most important were Zhengzhou and Anyang, which had palaces and temples surrounded by houses and workshops.

Developments in pottery making, such as the use of kilns, allowed Chinese potters to make beautiful red and black vases.

Mesopotamia and Egypt

The world's first cities developed in southern Mesopotamia around 3500 BCE. The city of Ur, which stood on the Euphrates River, grew into a thriving commercial center. As its power grew, the city took over neighboring villages and surrounding land, becoming a small kingdom. Neighboring Uruk was another important early city. Outside the walls, farmers grew barley, sesame, and onions, as well as raising sheep, goats, and cattle. In Egypt, fortified towns began to appear along the Nile. Later, they were unified by the first pharaoh in c. 3100 BCE. Giza, Memphis, and Saqqara were among the most important sites.

In the Indus Valley

Major farming settlements on the fertile land of the Indus floodplain (in present-day Pakistan) eventually grew into two great cities, Mohenjo-Daro and Harappa. They were well planned, with streets laid out in a grid pattern. Their mud-brick houses had washrooms and lavatories, and these were connected to drains that ran beneath the streets.

Painted terra-cotta pottery from Harappa. As village farming communities developed pottery became more sophisticated.

FARMING COMMUNITIES AND URBAN AREAS IN 2500 BCE

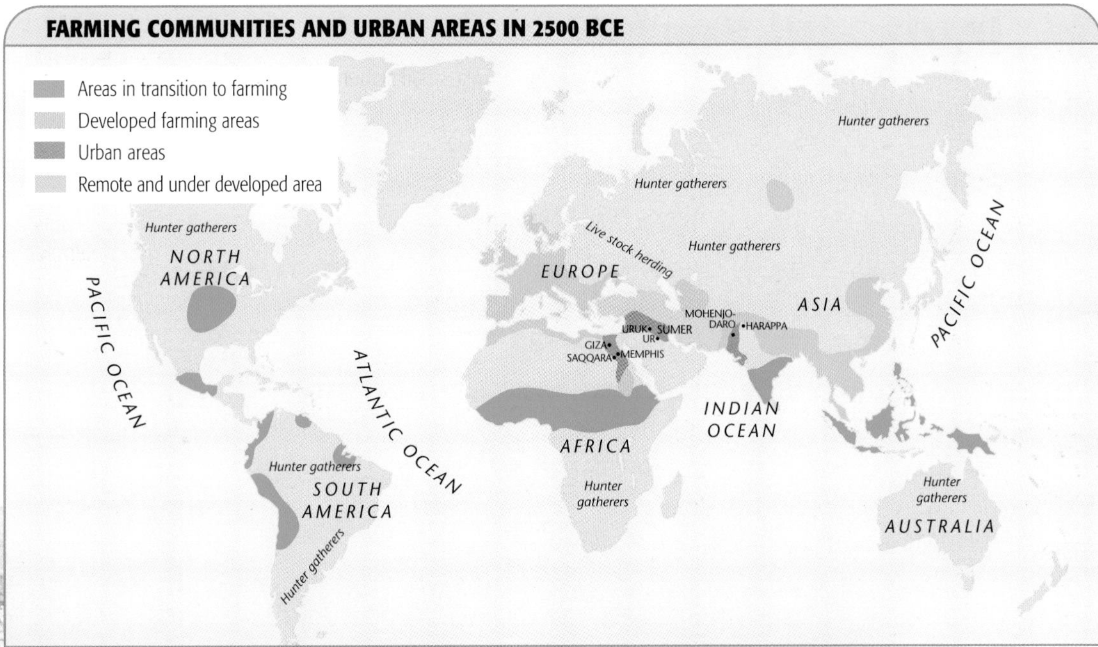

Development of Urban Areas

As people began making the transition from hunting and gathering to agriculture, villages of settled farmers gradually developed into larger urban areas or cities. This map of the world shows how areas of North America, South America, Central America, Africa, and Asia were still in the early stages of farming development in 2500 BCE while urban areas had already formed in Mesopotamia, the Indus Valley, and Egypt.

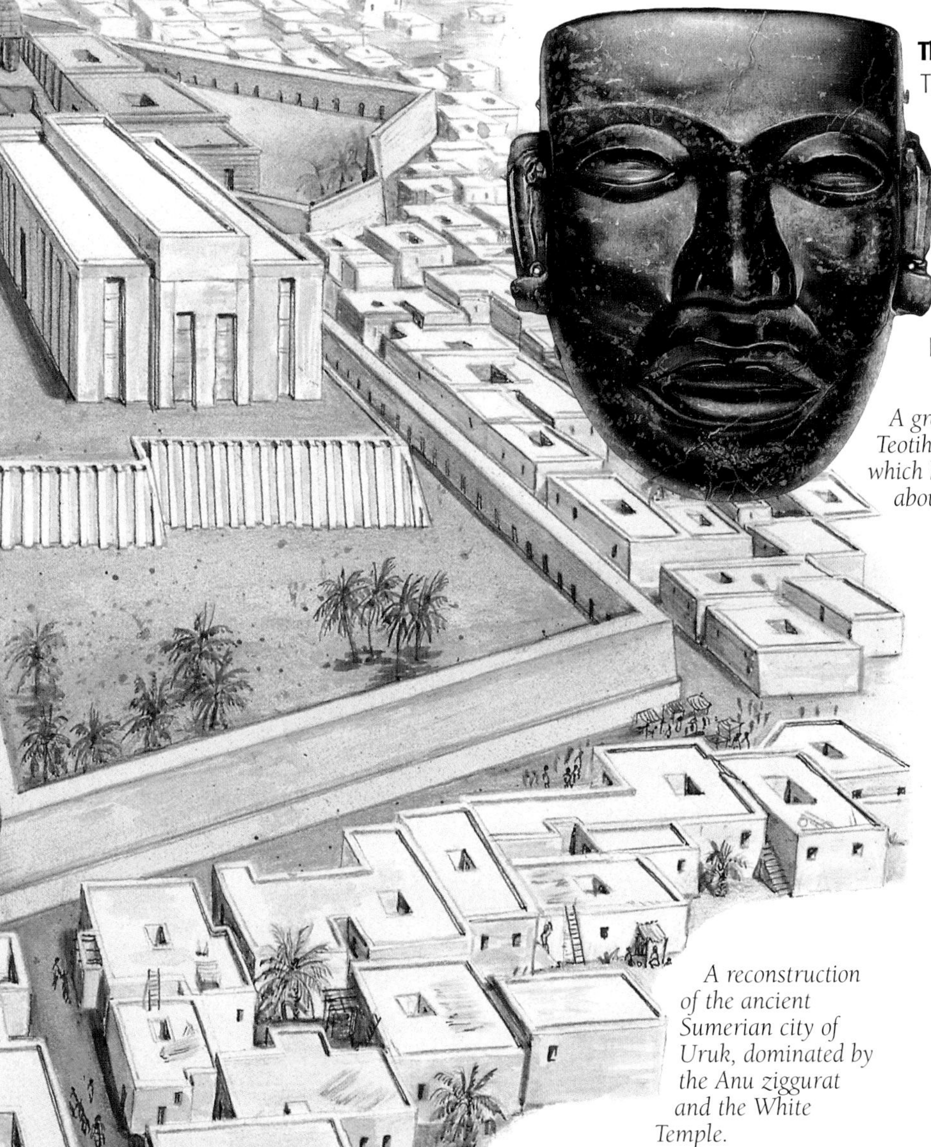

A reconstruction of the ancient Sumerian city of Uruk, dominated by the Anu ziggurat and the White Temple.

The Americas

The city of Monte Alban, in modern-day Mexico, was founded by the Zapotecs in 500 BCE when they leveled off the top of a mountain. The founders must have had contact with the Olmecs (see page 35), and by 200 BCE about 15,000 people were living around the ceremonial center of their city. In North America, the largest city grew at Cahokia around 800 CE, beside the Mississippi River in present-day Illinois. At its height, Cahokia had a population of up to 30,000.

A greenstone mask from the city of Teotihuacan, in the Valley of Mexico, which by 100 CE had a population of about 60,000.

Painted baked clay statuette of the Snake Goddess from Knossos.

Europe

Europe's first cities developed on the Mediterranean island of Crete over 4,000 years ago. They were built by the Minoans, who were so called after their legendary King Minos. The Minoans built large palace cities. The great palace city at Knossos had as many as 1,500 rooms. By 2000 BCE there were many other palace cities on Crete, including Phaistos, Mallia, and Zakro.

Protecting Trade

The early city-states that controlled trade had great power and did everything they could to protect their position. Cities such as Troy (on the coast of modern Turkey), which watched over trade between the Mediterranean and Black seas, were heavily protected but constantly attacked. Trade routes also had to be defended, and since they often ran through rival territories, overzealous protection sometimes led to disagreements and warfare.

Copper axe from Ur, about 2500 BCE. Such weapons may have been carried by royal guards.

Trade and Warfare

By 2000 BCE a long-distance trading system was developing around Mesopotamia. Since cities developed in river valleys, much of the transport was by water — along rivers and following coastlines on the open sea. Long before the first coins were minted, trade was carried out by exchanging goods. These included valuable and luxury items, such as metals and gemstones. The new trade routes led to communication between growing cities and smaller settlements in neighboring regions. Before long a trading network covered an extensive region from the Mediterranean Sea to the Indus Valley.

Mesopotamian professional soldiers rode off to battle in chariots drawn by asses. The invention of these vehicles revolutionised warfare.

Armies

The kings or other rulers of city-states generally acted as supreme commanders of their armies, often leading their troops into battle. There was usually a permanent standing army, paid for by the king, though military campaigns were usually organized after the harvest had been safely gathered. Troops carried shields and most foot soldiers were armed with spears. Spearmen also rode in chariots, and were replaced by archers in later more maneuvrable models.

This carving shows helmeted troops of the city-state of Lagash, in modern southern Iraq, moving against neighboring Umma about 2560 BCE. Both cities lay between trade routes that ran from the Persian Gulf.

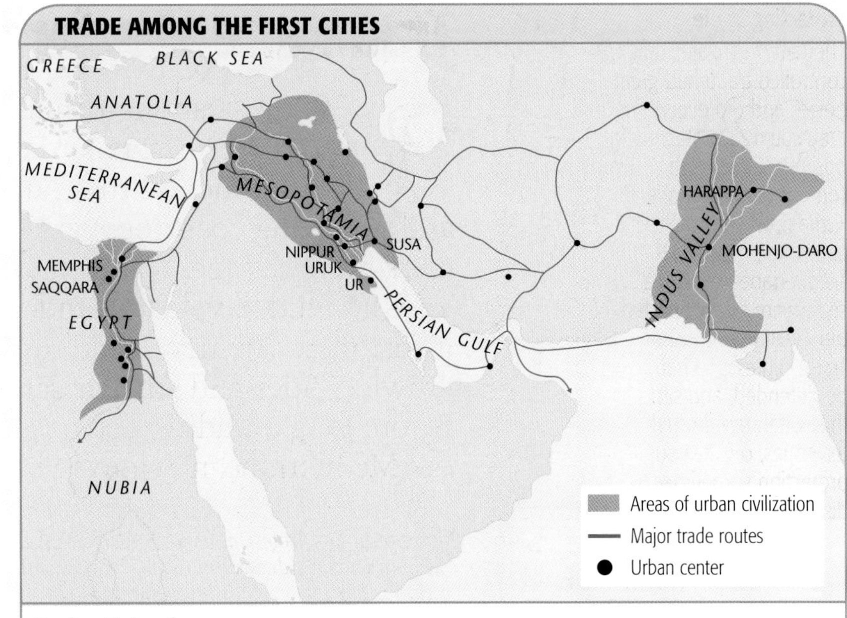

Trading Networks

The earliest cities and states set up trading networks. As well as trading with each other, Mesopotamian city-states engaged in trade with Indus valley cities such as Mohenjo-Daro. An overland trade route passed through Susa, while a sea route passed through the Persian Gulf. Shipbuilding, the domestication of the horse and camel, and the development of wheeled vehicles all helped to advance trade.

Valuable Goods

Much early trade between regions was in useful materials that were not available everywhere. A good example is obsidian, a black volcanic glass that was used for arrowheads and knives before the use of copper and bronze. Areas rich in minerals and metals were at a natural advantage. Gold and silver were valued for their beauty and rarity, and the Egyptians mined for gold in southern Nubia from early times. Hard green jade was used for making useful axes and musical instruments, as well as for beautiful jewelry and ornaments.

This jade mask made by Zapotecs, dating from about 200 BCE, is thought to represent a bat or a jaguar.

Chlorite vessel with stone inlay found in Nippur. It may have been made in modern-day Iran and brought over by traders.

Exchange of Ideas

Ideas were exchanged as well as materials and goods. The first wheeled vehicles probably appeared in Mesopotamia around 3600 BCE, and knowledge of this extraordinary invention soon spread far and wide. The same was true of advances in metalwork, especially smelting methods, though many developments seem to have appeared independently at different times in various places.

In Mesopotamia, writing was carved onto clay tablets. Important tablets were left to harden in the sun so they could be preserved and stored in libraries.

The Invention of Writing

People started writing about 5,500 years ago, when traders began using special marks to keep records and business accounts. The marks were made up of small pictures and symbols, and different writing systems arose in various cultures. The invention of writing, at a time when civilization was developing around the world, marked the end of prehistory. From that time on, people were able to record all their transactions, laws, and stories. This was the beginning of written history.

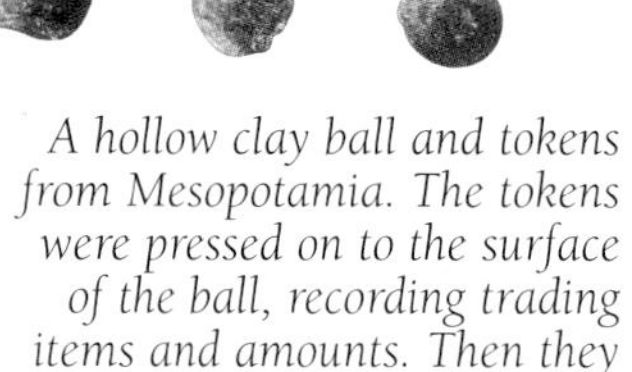

A hollow clay ball and tokens from Mesopotamia. The tokens were pressed on to the surface of the ball, recording trading items and amounts. Then they were sealed inside.

Cuneiform

The first writing system probably developed from clay tokens made by early Mesopotamian traders. By 3500 BCE the tokens were being kept in clay balls, and a few hundred years later the Mesopotamians began using reed stems to make wedge-shaped marks on wet clay tablets. The marks developed into a script called cuneiform (meaning "wedge-shaped") which was used for about 3,000 years to record important events.

Hieroglyphics

By about 3250 BCE the Egyptians were using a writing system that we call hieroglyphics (meaning "sacred carving"). This script used a mixture of picture symbols, sound signs (such as an owl for the letter "m"), and other symbols. It was used mainly for writing inscriptions in tombs and temples, and fewer than one in every hundred Egyptians could read or write the script. This meant that scribes played an important part in Egyptian life, working mainly for rulers and priests.

Oracle Bones

The earliest examples of Chinese writing are engraved on animal bones or pieces of tortoise shell. The bones and shells were heated until they cracked, and the pattern of cracks was seen as a message from ancestral spirits. The questions and answers were then inscribed on the bones with sharp metal pens.

Ancient oracle bones from Shang China, inscribed with pictographs.

This papyrus contains a hieroglyphic hymn to the hawk-headed sun-god Ra. Such writings were placed in coffins to help dead people on their way to the afterlife.

WRITING AROUND THE WORLD

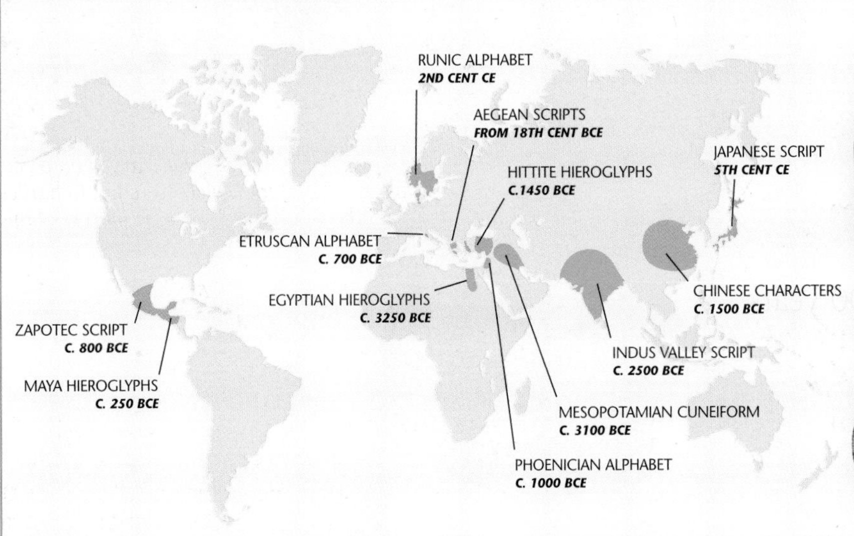

Writing Systems

We know that separate writing systems appeared at different times in various parts of the world, but we are not sure how much one system influenced another. It could be that the idea of writing spread from one culture to another, especially through trade, but that individual scripts arose independently.

WRITING HISTORY

c. 3500 BCE
The earliest form of writing, which developed into cuneiform, is used in Mesopotamia.

c. 3250 BCE
The Egyptians use hieroglyphic script.

c. 2500 BCE
Pictographs, writing in the form of pictures and drawings, are used in the Indus Valley.

c. 2300 BCE
The Akkadian language is written in cuneiform.

c. 1700 BCE
The Minoans write in so-called Linear A, a script that we still cannot understand.

c. 1500 BCE
Chinese pictographic writing on bones and shells; though some characters have changed, the basic system is still the same, making Chinese the oldest writing system still in use.

c. 1200 BCE
The Phoenicians use a 22-letter alphabet to write their Semitic language; this is later adopted by the ancient Greeks and so is the ancestor of all Western alphabets.

c. 800 BCE
Hieroglyphic script is developed in Central America.

This statuette shows a female Mayan scribe with a folded codex book.

Central America

In Central America the Zapotecs (see page 41) developed a hieroglyphic script around 800 BCE. All the later scripts of the region developed from this, including Mayan writing. The Maya wrote on thin strips of fig-tree bark, which they folded up like an accordion to make pages. We call these books codices.

Glossary

Abstract Term used to describe a simplified representation of objects, showing them as they do not appear in reality.

Aeon (also spelt eon) A unit of time too long to measure. A unit of time in the history of the world which is broken down into smaller units called eras.

Archeology The science which studies the remains of ancient peoples, such as tools, weapons, pots, and buildings, to learn more about cultures of the distant past.

Bacteria Small forms of life composed of a single cell that can be seen only with a microscope, usually found in decaying matter.

Bipedal Term used to describe animals that walk on their hind limbs.

Carnivore An animal that eats meat.

Comet A celestial body, composed mainly of gases, which circles around the Sun. When close enough to the Sun, it appears as a dense, bright mass surrounded by a misty light that forms a tail shape.

Composite Made up of two or more parts.

Cranium Bones, or part of the skull that covers the brain.

Crop A plant or its product, such as grain, fruit, or vegetables, grown by farmers.

Debris The remains or small pieces of anything that has broken up or been destroyed.

Dolmen A simple structure made of upright stones which support a large stone slab.

Domesticate To tame and bring animals and plants under control so that they can live with and be of use to people.

Dyke A thick wall built to hold back the flow of water.

Dynasty A line of rulers coming from the same family, or a period during which they reign.

Embankment A wall made of earth and or stones built to keep the waters of a river from overflowing.

Epoch A unit of time in the history of the Earth during which specific events or development occurs. Two or more epochs make up a period.

Era A set of years or a unit of time in the history of the Earth beginning and ending at specific point in time, usually characterized by particular circumstances or events. An era is made up of two or more periods.

Extinct Term used to describe species of animals or plants that have died out.

Forage To search for and collect food.

Fossil The remains or trace of an organism of the distant past, such as a hardened part or an imprint, embedded in the Earth's crust.

Galaxy A group of billions of stars which, together with gas and dust, forms a luminous band or cloud. The Sun and the Earth, along with the other planets, lie in the galaxy called the Milky Way.

Geological Term used to describe anything of or pertaining to the Earth's history.

Herbivore An animal that eats only plants.

Hierarchy A classification system in which people or things are given higher and lower rank or importance.

Hominid A human-like primate which walks on two legs. The only hominid species alive today is *Homo sapiens*, the species to which modern humans belong.

Ice Age A period of Earth's history in which huge sheets of ice cover a vast part of the Earth's surface.

Irrigation The process of bringing water to fields.

Leverage The mechanical advantage gained by using a lever, a simple tool centered on a fixed point and used to raise or move objects placed at one end by pushing down on the other.

Lintel A piece of stone or wood which makes up the top part of a doorway or window frame.

Mammal A type of animal which, when young, feeds off milk from its mother's body. There are three major groups of mammals; monotremes, marsupials, and placentals.

Marrow The soft, fatty material found in the centre of bones.

Marsupial A kind of mammal which spends the early years of its life inside a pouch on the skin of its mother's body.

Megalith A huge stone, usually standing, used in the construction of prehistoric monuments.

Meteorite A mass of stone or metal which has fallen upon the Earth from space.

Molten Melted, or in a liquid state under a very high temperature.

Monotreme A primitive egg-laying mammal.

Ore Rock or earth from which a precious or useful metal can be obtained.

Period One of the units of time which make up an era. Periods are broken down into smaller units of time called epochs.

Pigment Any colored substance used to make paint or a colored mixture. A natural substance which gives color to plants and animals.

Placental A kind of mammal which develops and is nourished inside its mother's body by an organ called the placenta.

Plowshare A sharp metal wedge used to turn over the top layer of soil.

Primate A highly developed placental mammal with flexible hands and feet and a large brain.

Scavenger An animal which feeds off dead, decaying animals.

Smelting The process of melting down earth (or an ore) in order to separate and extract its metallic parts.

Species A group of related organisms which share important characteristics and are given a common name. An organism belonging to such a group.

Toggle A short wooden stick or bar.

Ziggurat An ancient Mesopotamian stepped pyramid-like structure with a temple on top.

Index